Published by Pearson Education Limited, 80 Strand, London, WC2R 0RL
www.pearsonschoolsandfecolleges.co.uk
Text © Pearson Education Limited 2017
Editorial management by Gwladys Rushworth for Haremi
Edited by Fabienne Tartarin
Typeset by York Publishing Solutions Pvt. Ltd.
Cover image: Shutterstock.com/Sergey Kelin
Cover © Pearson Education Limited 2017

Written by Angela Stanley

First published 2017
10 9 8
2022

British Library Cataloguing in Publication Data
A catalogue record for this book is available from the British Library.
ISBN 978 1 292 17257 6

Copyright notice
All rights reserved. No part of this publication may be reproduced in any form or by any means (including photocopying or storing it in any medium by electronic means and whether or not transiently or incidentally to some other use of this publication) without the written permission of the copyright owner, except in accordance with the provisions of the Copyright, Design and Patents Act 1988 or under the terms of a license issued by the Copyright Licensing Agency, Barnard's Inn, 86 Fetter Lane, London EC4A 1EN (www.cla.co.uk). Applications for the copyright owner's written permission should be addressed to the publisher.

Printed in the UK by Ashford Colour Press

Contenu

High-frequency words **4**

Module 1
Words I should know for speaking and writing activities **15**
Extra words I should know for reading and listening activities **18**

Module 2
Words I should know for speaking and writing activities **19**
Extra words I should know for reading and listening activities **22**

Module 3
Words I should know for speaking and writing activities **23**
Extra words I should know for reading and listening activities **26**

Module 4
Words I should know for speaking and writing activities **27**
Extra words I should know for reading and listening activities **30**

Module 5
Words I should know for speaking and writing activities **31**
Extra words I should know for reading and listening activities **34**

Module 6
Words I should know for speaking and writing activities **35**
Extra words I should know for reading and listening activities **38**

Module 7
Words I should know for speaking and writing activities **40**
Extra words I should know for reading and listening activities **43**

Module 8
Words I should know for speaking and writing activities **44**
Extra words I should know for reading and listening activities **47**

High-frequency words

Common –er verbs

accepter	to accept
adorer	to love, to adore
aider	to help
aimer	to like
aller	to go
aller à pied	to walk
allumer	to light, to turn, to switch on
améliorer	to improve
(s)'arrêter	to stop

Had a look ☐ Nearly there ☐ Nailed it ☐

chanter	to sing
chercher	to look for
cliquer	to click (ICT)
coller	to stick
commander	to order
compter/compter sur	to count, to intend, to count on (someone)
contacter	to contact
continuer	to continue, to carry on
copier	to copy
se coucher	to go to bed
coûter	to cost

Had a look ☐ Nearly there ☐ Nailed it ☐

se débrouiller	to cope, to manage, to get by
décider	to decide
décoller	to take off (plane)
se dépêcher	to hurry
dépenser	to spend (money)
se déshabiller	to get undressed
désirer	to want, to desire
dessiner	to draw
détester	to hate
discuter	to discuss
donner	to give
durer	to last

Had a look ☐ Nearly there ☐ Nailed it ☐

s'échapper	to escape
écouter	to listen
écraser	to squash
empêcher	to prevent
endommager	to harm, to damage
entrer	to enter, to go in
envoyer	to send
espérer	to hope
essayer	to try
étudier	to study
expliquer	to explain

Had a look ☐ Nearly there ☐ Nailed it ☐

se fâcher	to get angry
fermer	to close, to switch off
frapper	to knock, to hit
gagner	to earn, to win
garder	to look after, to mind (child, dog)
garer	to park
gérer	to manage (business)
s'habiller	to get dressed
habiter	to live (inhabit)
informer	to inform
inviter	to invite
jeter	to throw

Had a look ☐ Nearly there ☐ Nailed it ☐

laisser	to leave behind (an object)
(se) laver	to wash
se lever	to get up
louer	to rent, to hire
manger	to eat
manquer	to miss, to be lacking
marcher	to walk, to work (function)
mériter	to deserve
monter	to climb, to get on(to), to go up
monter (dans)	to get into (bus, car, train)
montrer	to show
nettoyer	to clean
noter	to note

Had a look ☐ Nearly there ☐ Nailed it ☐

s'occuper de	to look after
organiser	to organise
ôter	to take off (clothes etc.)
oublier	to forget, to leave something behind
pardonner	to forgive
parler	to speak
passer	to pass, to spend (time)
penser	to think (about)

High-frequency words

peser	to weigh	tomber	to fall
pleurer	to cry	toucher	to touch
porter	to wear	travailler	to work
poser	to place	traverser	to cross, to go across
pousser	to push	trouver	to find
préférer	to prefer		
présenter	to introduce (a person), to present		

Had a look ☐ **Nearly there** ☐ **Nailed it** ☐

prêter	to lend	utiliser	to use
se promener	to go for a walk	vérifier	to check
quitter	to leave (somewhere, somebody)	voler	to fly, to steal
		voyager	to travel

Had a look ☐ **Nearly there** ☐ **Nailed it** ☐   **Had a look** ☐ **Nearly there** ☐ **Nailed it** ☐

raconter	to tell, to recount	**Common –ir verbs**	
se rappeler	to remember	atterrir	to land
rater	to fail, to miss (train, bus, etc.)	choisir	to choose
		s'endormir	to fall asleep
rechercher	to research	finir	to finish, to end
recommander	to recommend	nourrir	to feed, to nourish
regretter	to regret, to be sorry	offrir	to offer, to give a present/gift
rembourser	to refund		
remercier	to thank	ouvrir	to open
remplacer	to replace	partir	to leave, to depart
rencontrer	to meet	prévenir	to warn
rentrer (à la maison)	to return (home), to go back (home)	remplir	to fill, to fill in
		réussir	to succeed
renverser	to knock over	se servir de	to use
réparer	to repair	sortir	to go out
répéter	to repeat	se souvenir	to remember
se reposer	to rest	tenir	to hold
réserver	to reserve	venir	to come
ressembler	to look like, to resemble		
rester	to stay		
retourner (à l'école)	to return (to school), to go back (to school)		

Had a look ☐ **Nearly there** ☐ **Nailed it** ☐

		Common –re verbs	
se réveiller	to wake up	apprendre	to learn
rouler	to go (in a car)	attendre	to wait for

Had a look ☐ **Nearly there** ☐ **Nailed it** ☐   boire — to drink

		conduire	to drive
sauter	to jump	connaître	to know (person, place)
sauver	to save	décrire	to describe
sembler	to seem	descendre (de)	to get out of (bus, car, train)
signer	to sign	dire	to tell, to say
signifier	to mean, to signify	entendre	to hear
sonner	to ring (a bell)	éteindre	to switch off
souhaiter	to wish	(se) faire mal	to hurt (oneself)
stationner	to park	introduire	to introduce (an item, an idea)
téléphoner	to phone		
(se) terminer	to end	lire	to read
tirer	to pull		

Had a look ☐ **Nearly there** ☐ **Nailed it** ☐

5

High-frequency words

mettre	to put
plaire (à)	to please
prendre	to take
produire	to produce
remettre	to put back
répondre	to reply
rire	to laugh
sourire	to smile
suivre	to follow
vivre	to live
vendre	to sell

Had a look ☐ **Nearly there** ☐ **Nailed it** ☐

Common –*oir* verbs

avoir	to have
avoir besoin de	to need
avoir l'intention de (faire)	to mean to (do)
devoir	to have to, to must
savoir	to know (a fact)
voir	to see
vouloir	to want

Had a look ☐ **Nearly there** ☐ **Nailed it** ☐

Common adjectives: describing someone

actif/-ve	active
agréable	pleasant
amical(e)	friendly
bavard(e)	talkative
bête	silly
calme	peaceful, quiet, calm
désagréable	unpleasant
drôle	funny (comical)
égoïste	selfish
généreux/-euse	generous
gentil(le)	kind
gros(se)	fat
honnête	honest
indépendant(e)	independent
intelligent(e)	intelligent, clever
joli(e)	pretty
laid(e)	ugly
marrant(e)	funny (comical)
méchant(e)	naughty
mince	slim

Had a look ☐ **Nearly there** ☐ **Nailed it** ☐

moche	ugly
mûr(e)	mature
optimiste	optimistic
paresseux/-euse	lazy
(im)patient(e)	(im)patient
pessimiste	pessimistic
petit(e)	small, short (person)
(im)poli(e)	(im)polite
populaire	popular
responsable	responsible
rigolo(te)	funny (comical)
sage	good (well-behaved), wise
sérieux/-euse	serious
sévère	strict
strict(e)	strict
sympa (invariable)	nice, likeable
sympathique	nice, likeable
timide	shy
travailleur/-euse	hard-working
vilain(e)	naughty

Had a look ☐ **Nearly there** ☐ **Nailed it** ☐

Common adjectives: I am, you are, we are ...

célèbre	famous
content(e)	pleased
de bonne humeur	in a good mood
étonné(e)	surprised
faible (en maths, etc.)	weak (in maths, etc.)
fatigué(e)	tired
fort(e) (en maths, etc.)	strong (in maths, etc.)
heureux/-euse	happy, content
inquiet/-iète	worried
jeune	young
malheureux/-euse	unhappy
perdu(e)	lost
pressé(e)	in a hurry
reconnaissant(e)	grateful
riche	rich
satisfait(e)	satisfied
sauf/-ve	safe
surpris(e)	surprised
triste	sad
vieux/vieil/vieille	old

Had a look ☐ **Nearly there** ☐ **Nailed it** ☐

Common adjectives: opinions

amusant(e)	fun, amusing
bruyant(e)	noisy
cher/-ère	expensive
chouette	great (fantastic)
démodé(e)	old fashioned
dur(e)	hard
effrayant(e)	frightening

High-frequency words

facile	easy, simple	haut	high, tall (building)
fantastique	fantastic	léger/-ère	light
fatigant(e)	tiring	libre	free (unoccupied, available)
favori(te)	favourite	long(ue)	long
formidable	great (marvellous)	lourd(e)	heavy
génial(e)	great (fantastic)		

Had a look ☐ **Nearly there** ☐ **Nailed it** ☐

idéal(e)	ideal		
incroyable	unbelievable		
injuste	unfair	même	same
inutile	useless	moderne	modern
juste	fair	mouillé(e)	wet
		mûr(e)	ripe

Had a look ☐ **Nearly there** ☐ **Nailed it** ☐

neuf/-ve	new (brand new)
nombreux/-euse	numerous
normal(e)	normal
nouveau/nouvel/nouvelle	new
ouvert(e)	open

magnifique	magnificent		
malsain(e)	unhealthy		
merveilleux/-euse	marvellous		
nécessaire	necessary		
négatif/-ve	negative		

Had a look ☐ **Nearly there** ☐ **Nailed it** ☐

parfait(e)	perfect		
passionnant(e)	exciting	pareil(le)	alike, the same
positif/-ve	positive	plein(e)	full
pratique	practical	pourri(e)	rotten
préféré(e)	favourite	prêt(e)	ready
raisonnable	reasonable	prochain(e)	next
ridicule	ridiculous	propre	own
sain(e)	healthy (food/way of life)	rangé(e)	tidy
sensationnel(le)	sensational	rapide	fast
sensass	sensational	récent(e)	recent
super	great (fantastic)	reconnu(e)	recognised, well known
simple	easy, simple	réel(le)	real
superbe	superb	silencieux/-ieuse	silent
utile	useful	situé(e)	situated
valable	valid	tranquille	peaceful, quiet, calm
vrai(e)	true	type	typical

Had a look ☐ **Nearly there** ☐ **Nailed it** ☐   **Had a look** ☐ **Nearly there** ☐ **Nailed it** ☐

Other common adjectives

à la mode	fashionable
ancien(ne)	former, old
autre	other
chaud(e)	hot
court(e)	short
d'une grande valeur	valuable
dernier/-ière	last
étroit(e)	thin, narrow
fermé à clef	locked
grand(e)	large, big
gratuit(e)	free (at no cost)
grave	serious
gros(se)	large, big

Comparisons/Superlatives

plus/moins	more/less
plus que/moins que	more than/less than
bon/meilleur/le meilleur	good/better/best
mauvais/pire/le pire	bad/worse/worst
bien/mieux/le mieux	well/better/best
mal/plus mal/le plus mal	badly/worse/worst
beaucoup/plus/le plus	a lot, lots/more/the most
peu/moins/le moins	few, little/less/the least

Had a look ☐ **Nearly there** ☐ **Nailed it** ☐

Common adverbs

à peine	hardly
assez	fairly, quite

High-frequency words

aussi	too, as well	au fond	in the background, at the back
trop	too		
bien	well	au fond de	at the back of, at the bottom of
bientôt	soon		
bon marché	cheap(ly)	au lieu de	instead of
d'habitude	usually	au milieu (de)	in the middle (of)
debout	standing	au premier plan	in the foreground
déjà	already	au-dessus de	above
encore	again	autour de	around
ensemble	together	avant	before
fort	loud(ly)	avec	with
(mal)heureusement	(un)fortunately	chez	at (someone's house)
ici	here	contre	against
immédiatement	immediately	dans	in (inside)
jamais	never	de	from
là	there	dehors	outside
là-bas	over there		
là-haut	up there		
longtemps	(for) a long time		

Had a look ☐ **Nearly there** ☐ **Nailed it** ☐

		depuis	since, for
		derrière	behind
		devant	in front of, in the front
normalement	usually	en	in, within (time)
nulle part	nowhere	en dehors de	outside (of)
partout	everywhere	en face de	opposite
pas encore	not yet	en haut	above
peut-être	perhaps	en-dessous	under/underneath
plutôt	rather	entre	between
presque	almost	jusqu'à	until
quelque part	somewhere	loin de	far from
quelquefois	sometimes	malgré	despite, in spite of
rarement	rarely	nulle part	nowhere
récemment	recently	par	through
souvent	often	parmi	among(st)
surtout	especially	pour	for, in order to
toujours	always, still	près (de)	near (to)
tout de suite	straight away, immediately	sans	without
très	very	selon	according to
vite	quickly	sous	under/underneath
vraiment	really	sur	on (on top of)
		vers	towards

Had a look ☐ **Nearly there** ☐ **Nailed it** ☐

Had a look ☐ **Nearly there** ☐ **Nailed it** ☐

Prepositions

à	at, to
à côté de	next to
à partir de	from
à travers	across
après	after
au bord de	at the side/edge of
au bout de	at the end of

Connectives

à cause de	because of
à part	apart from
ainsi	so, therefore
alors	so, therefore, then
aussi	also
car	because
cependant	however

High-frequency words

c'est-à-dire	that is to say, i.e.	vingt-trois	23
comme	as, like	vingt-quatre	24
d'un côté/de l'autre côté	on the one hand/on the other hand	vingt-cinq	25
		vingt-six	26
donc	so, therefore	vingt-sept	27

Had a look ☐ **Nearly there** ☐ **Nailed it** ☐

		vingt-huit	28
		vingt-neuf	29
		trente	30
ensuite	next	trente et un	31
évidemment	obviously	trente-deux, etc.	32, etc.
mais	but	quarante	40
même si	even if	cinquante	50
ou	or	soixante	60
par contre	on the other hand		

Had a look ☐ **Nearly there** ☐ **Nailed it** ☐

par exemple	for example		
pendant que	while		
pourtant	however	soixante-dix	70
puis	then	soixante et onze	71
puisque	seeing that, since	soixante-douze	72
quand	when	soixante-treize	73
sans doute	undoubtedly, without doubt, probably	soixante-quatorze	74
		soixante-quinze	75
si	if	soixante-seize	76
y compris	including	soixante-dix-sept	77

Had a look ☐ **Nearly there** ☐ **Nailed it** ☐

soixante-dix-huit	78
soixante-dix-neuf	79

Had a look ☐ **Nearly there** ☐ **Nailed it** ☐

Numbers

un(e)	1
deux	2
trois	3
quatre	4
cinq	5
six	6
sept	7
huit	8
neuf	9
dix	10
onze	11
douze	12
treize	13
quatorze	14
quinze	15
seize	16
dix-sept	17
dix-huit	18
dix-neuf	19

quatre-vingts	80
quatre-vingt-un	81
quatre-vingt-deux, etc.	82, etc.
quatre-vingt-dix	90
quatre-vingt-onze	91
quatre-vingt-douze, etc.	92, etc.

Had a look ☐ **Nearly there** ☐ **Nailed it** ☐

cent (m)	100
cent un(e)	101
cent vingt	120
deux cents	200
mille (m)	1000
mille cent	1100
deux mille	2000
un million (m)	1,000,000
deux millions (m)	2,000,000
premier/-ière	first
deuxième	second
onzième	eleventh
vingt-et-unième	twenty first

Had a look ☐ **Nearly there** ☐ **Nailed it** ☐

vingt	20
vingt et un	21
vingt-deux	22

Had a look ☐ **Nearly there** ☐ **Nailed it** ☐

High-frequency words

Opinions

à mon avis	in my opinion
absolument	absolutely
bien entendu	of course
bien sûr	of course
ça dépend	that depends
ça m'énerve	it gets on my nerves
ça me fait rire	it makes me laugh
ça me plaît	I like it
ça m'est égal	it's all the same to me
ça ne me dit rien	it means nothing to me, I don't fancy that, I don't feel like it
ça suffit	that's enough
ça ne fait rien	it doesn't matter
ce n'est pas la peine	it's not worth it
d'accord	OK (in agreement)
j'en ai assez/marre	I've had enough
personnellement	personally

Had a look ☐   Nearly there ☐   Nailed it ☐

Other useful expressions

à bientôt	see you soon
à demain/vendredi	see you tomorrow/on Friday
bonne chance	good luck
bon courage	good luck
Ça s'écrit comment?	How do you spell that?
ça va	I'm fine, it's OK
comme çi, comme ça	so-so
désolé(e)	sorry
défense de	you are not allowed to
dommage	what a shame
excuse-/excusez-moi	(I'm) sorry (informal/formal)
il est interdit de	you are not allowed to

Had a look ☐   Nearly there ☐   Nailed it ☐

il faut	you must/one must
il y a	there is/are
je ne comprends pas	I don't understand
je ne sais pas	I don't know
merci (bien)	thank you (very much)
Qu'est-ce que cela veut dire?	What does that mean?
avec plaisir	with pleasure
tant mieux	all/so much the better
tant pis	too bad
voici	here is/are
voilà	there is/are (i.e. over there)
volontiers	with pleasure

Had a look ☐   Nearly there ☐   Nailed it ☐

Other useful little words

ça/cela	that
le chiffre	figure (number)
la chose	thing
comme	as, like
la façon	way (manner)
la fois	time (occasion)
le genre	type (kind of)
madame	Mrs, Madam
mademoiselle	Miss
monsieur	Mr, Sir
le nombre	number
le numéro	number (phone number)
par exemple	for example
quelqu'un	someone
quelque chose	something
sauf	except
la sorte	type (kind of)
tout le monde	everybody

Had a look ☐   Nearly there ☐   Nailed it ☐

Time, frequency and sequencing expressions

à ... heure(s)	at ... o'clock
à ... heure(s) et quart	at quarter past ...
à ... heure(s) et demie	at half past ...
à ... heure(s) moins le quart	at quarter to ...
à la fois	at the same time
à l'avenir	in future, from now on
à l'heure	on time
à temps partiel	part-time
l'an (m)	year
l'année (f)	year
après	after
après-demain	the day after tomorrow
après-midi	afternoon
aujourd'hui	today
auparavant	formerly, in the past
avant	before
avant-hier	the day before yesterday
bientôt	soon

Had a look ☐   Nearly there ☐   Nailed it ☐

d'abord	at first, firstly
dans le futur	in the future
d'habitude	usually
de bonne heure	early
le début	start
demain	tomorrow

High-frequency words

dernier/dernière	last
de temps en temps	from time to time
déjà	already
de nouveau	again
en attendant	whilst waiting (for), meanwhile
en avance	in advance
en ce moment	at the moment
en retard	late
en train de (faire…)	(to be) doing
en même temps	at the same time
encore une fois	once more, again
enfin	at last, finally
environ	about, approximately

Had a look ☐ Nearly there ☐ Nailed it ☐

la fin	end
hier	yesterday
il y a	ago
le jour	day
la journée	day
le lendemain	the next day
longtemps	for a long time
maintenant	now
le matin	morning
le mois	month
normalement	normally
la nuit	night
parfois	sometimes
le passé	past
pendant	during
plus tard	later
presque	almost, nearly
prochain	next

Had a look ☐ Nearly there ☐ Nailed it ☐

quelquefois	sometimes
rarement	rarely
récemment	recently
la semaine	week
seulement	only
le siècle	century
le soir	evening
soudain	suddenly
souvent	often
suivant	following
sur le point de (être)	(to be) about to
tard	late
tôt	early
toujours	always, still
tous les jours	every day

tout à coup	suddenly, all of a sudden
tout de suite	immediately
vite	quickly

Had a look ☐ Nearly there ☐ Nailed it ☐

Question words

Comment?	How?
Combien (de)?	How much, How many?
Que?	What?
Qu'est-ce qui?	What? (as subject)
Qu'est-ce que?	What? (as object)
Quoi?	What?
De quelle couleur?	What colour?
Comment?	What like?
À quelle heure?	(At) what time?
Quel/Quelle?	What/which?
Quand?	When?
Où?	Where?
Lequel/Laquelle/ Lesquels/Lesquelles?	Which one(s)?
Qui?	Who?
Pourquoi?	Why?

Had a look ☐ Nearly there ☐ Nailed it ☐

Colours

blanc(he)	white
bleu(e)	blue
brun(e)	brown
châtain (invariable)	chestnut brown
clair(e)	light
foncé(e)	dark
gris(e)	grey
jaune	yellow
marron (invariable)	brown, chestnut brown
noir(e)	black
rose	pink
rouge	red
vert(e)	green
violet(te)	violet

Had a look ☐ Nearly there ☐ Nailed it ☐

Days, months and seasons of the year

lundi	Monday
mardi	Tuesday
mercredi	Wednesday
jeudi	Thursday
vendredi	Friday
samedi	Saturday
dimanche	Sunday

Had a look ☐ Nearly there ☐ Nailed it ☐

High-frequency words

le mois	month	un pot (de)	a jar (of)
janvier	January	une boîte (de)	a tin, (of), a box (of)
février	February	une bouteille (de)	a bottle (of)
mars	March	une centaine (de)	about a hundred
avril	April	une douzaine (de)	a dozen
mai	May	une tranche (de)	a slice (of)
juin	June	une vingtaine (de)	about twenty
juillet	July		
août	August		
septembre	September		
octobre	October		
novembre	November		
décembre	December		

Had a look ☐ Nearly there ☐ Nailed it ☐

la saison	season
(en) automne (m)	(in) autumn
(au) printemps (m)	(in) spring
(en) été (m)	(in) summer
(en) hiver (m)	(in) winter

Had a look ☐ Nearly there ☐ Nailed it ☐

Countries

l'Algérie (f)	Algeria
l'Allemagne (f)	Germany
l'Angleterre (f)	England
l'Autriche (f)	Austria
la Belgique	Belgium
le Canada	Canada
la Chine	China
le Danemark	Denmark
la France	France
la Grande-Bretagne	Great Britain
la Grèce	Greece
la Hollande	Holland

Had a look ☐ Nearly there ☐ Nailed it ☐

Quantities and measures

assez (de)	enough
beaucoup (de)	a lot (of), many
un centilitre	centilitre
un centimètre	centimetre
demi	half
une gramme	gramme
un kilomètre	kilometre
un mètre	metre
moins (de)	less
more encore (de)	(some)
pas mal (de)	quite a few
(un) peu (de)	a little of, few
plus (de)	more
plusieurs	several
le poids	weight
la quantité	quantity
un quart	quarter
quelques	some
un tiers	third
trop (de)	too much, too many

l'Inde (f)	India
l'Irlande (f)	Ireland
l'Italie (f)	Italy
les Pays-Bas	Netherlands
le Pakistan	Pakistan
la Russie	Russia
l'Écosse (f)	Scotland
le Sénégal	Senegal
l'Espagne (f)	Spain
la Suisse	Switzerland
la Tunisie	Tunisia
la Turquie	Turkey
le Royaume-Uni	United Kingdom
les États-Unis (m)	United States
le pays de Galles	Wales

Had a look ☐ Nearly there ☐ Nailed it ☐

Continents

l'Afrique (f)	Africa
l'Asie (f)	Asia
l'Australie (f)	Australia
l'Europe (f)	Europe
l'Amérique du Nord (f)	North America
l'Amérique du Sud (f)	South America

Had a look ☐ Nearly there ☐ Nailed it ☐

Had a look ☐ Nearly there ☐ Nailed it ☐

un kilo (de)	a kilo (of)
un litre (de)	a litre (of)
un morceau (de)	a piece (of)
un paquet (de)	a packet (of)
un peu (de)	a little (of)

High-frequency words

Nationalities
algérien(ne)	Algerian
allemand(e)	German
américain(e)	American
anglais(e)	English
autrichien(ne)	Austrian
belge	Belgian
britannique	British
canadien(ne)	Canadian
chinois(e)	Chinese
corse	Corsican
danois(e)	Danish
écossais(e)	Scottish
espagnol(e)	Spanish
européen(ne)	European
français(e)	French
gallois(e)	Welsh
grec(que)	Greek
hollandais(e)	Dutch

Had a look ☐ **Nearly there** ☐ **Nailed it** ☐

indien(ne)	Indian
irlandais(e)	Irish
italien(ne)	Italian
pakistanais(e)	Pakistani
russe	Russian
suisse	Swiss
tunisien(ne)	Tunisian
turque	Turkish

Had a look ☐ **Nearly there** ☐ **Nailed it** ☐

Geographical surroundings
à droite	on/to the right
à gauche	on/to the left
chez	at the house of
de chaque côté	from each side
de l'autre côté	from the other side
en bas	down(stairs)
en haut	up(stairs)
ici	here
là	there
là-bas	over there

Had a look ☐ **Nearly there** ☐ **Nailed it** ☐

la banlieue	suburb
la campagne	countryside
le centre-ville	town centre
la ville	town

Had a look ☐ **Nearly there** ☐ **Nailed it** ☐

loin de	far from
nulle part	nowhere
par	by
partout	everywhere
quelque part	somewhere
situé(e)	situated
tout droit	straight ahead
tout près	very near
toutes directions	all directions

Had a look ☐ **Nearly there** ☐ **Nailed it** ☐

l'est (m)	east
l'ouest (m)	west
le nord	north
le sud	south

Had a look ☐ **Nearly there** ☐ **Nailed it** ☐

Materials
l'argent (m)	silver
le béton	concrete
le bois	wood
le cuir	leather
le fer	iron
la laine	wool
l'or (m)	gold
la soie	silk
le verre	glass

Had a look ☐ **Nearly there** ☐ **Nailed it** ☐

Climate
l'averse (f)	shower
briller	to shine
le brouillard	fog
la brume	mist
la chaleur	heat
le ciel	sky
le climat	climate
couvert	overcast
doux	mild
l'éclair (m)	lightning
l'éclaircie (f)	bright spell
ensoleillé	sunny
faire beau	to be fine (weather)
faire mauvais	to be bad (weather)
geler	to freeze
la glace	ice
humide	humid, wet
la météo	weather forecast
mouillé	wet

Had a look ☐ **Nearly there** ☐ **Nailed it** ☐

13

High-frequency words

neiger	*to snow*
le nuage	*cloud*
nuageux	*cloudy*
l'ombre (f)	*shade, shadow*
l'orage (m)	*storm*
orageux	*stormy*
pleuvoir	*to rain*
la pluie	*rain*
sec	*dry*
la tempête	*storm*
le temps	*weather*
le tonnerre	*thunder*
tremper	*to soak*
le vent	*wind*

Had a look ☐ **Nearly there** ☐ **Nailed it** ☐

Social conventions

à plus tard	*see you later*
à tout à l'heure	*see you later*
allô	*hello (on the telephone)*
amitiés	*best wishes*
amuse-toi/amusez-vous bien!	*enjoy yourself/yourselves!*
au revoir	*goodbye*
au secours	*help!*
bien sûr	*of course*
bon voyage	*have a good journey*
bonjour	*hello, good morning*
bonne journée	*have a good day*
bonne nuit	*goodnight*
bonne soirée	*have a good evening*
bonsoir	*good evening*
de rien	*don't mention it*
Je t'/vous en prie	*It's a pleasure*
non merci	*no thank you*
pardon?	*I beg your pardon? Pardon?*
prière de	*please (request – formal)*
rendez-vous (m)	*meeting, meeting place*
rendez-vous à six heures	*meet you at 6 o'clock*
s'il te plaît/s'il vous plaît	*please (informal)/please (polite)*
salut	*hi*
veuillez	*please (request – formal)*

Had a look ☐ **Nearly there** ☐ **Nailed it** ☐

Module 1 Vocabulaire

Words I should know for speaking and writing activities

La famille	Family members
les parents (m)	parents
le père	father
la mère	mother
le beau-père	stepfather, father-in-law
la belle-mère	stepmother, mother-in-law
le mari	husband
la femme	wife
les enfants (m)	children
le fils	son
la fille	daughter
le frère	brother
la sœur	sister

Had a look ☐ **Nearly there** ☐ **Nailed it** ☐

le demi-frère	half-brother, stepbrother
la demi-sœur	half-sister, stepsister
le beau-frère	brother-in-law
la belle-sœur	sister-in-law
les grands-parents (m)	grandparents
le grand-père	grandfather
la grand-mère	grandmother
les petits-enfants (m)	grandchildren
le petit-fils	grandson
la petite-fille	granddaughter
l'oncle (m)	uncle
la tante	aunt
le cousin/la cousine	cousin

Had a look ☐ **Nearly there** ☐ **Nailed it** ☐

Les adjectifs de personnalité	Personality adjectives
Il/Elle est …	He/She is …
agaçant(e)	annoying
arrogant(e)	arrogant
amusant(e)	amusing, funny
bavard(e)	talkative, chatty
charmant(e)	charming
content(e)	happy
fort(e)	strong
impatient(e)	impatient
impoli(e)	impolite
indépendant(e)	independent
intelligent(e)	intelligent
marrant(e)	funny
méchant(e)	nasty, mean
têtu(e)	stubborn, pig-headed

Had a look ☐ **Nearly there** ☐ **Nailed it** ☐

Ma description physique	My physical description
J'ai les cheveux …	I have …
courts/longs	short/long hair
raides/bouclés/frisés	straight/curly hair
noirs/bruns/blonds	black/brown/blond hair
roux/gris/blancs	red/grey/white hair
J'ai les yeux …	I have …
bleus/verts	blue/green eyes
gris/marron	grey/brown eyes
J'ai …	I have …
des lunettes	glasses
des boutons	spots
une moustache	a moustache
une barbe	a beard
Je suis …	I am …
petit(e)/grand(e)	short/tall
de taille moyenne	of average height
mince/gros(se)	thin/fat

Had a look ☐ **Nearly there** ☐ **Nailed it** ☐

En ville	In town
la boîte de nuit	night club
le bowling	bowling alley
le café	café
le centre commercial	shopping centre
le cinéma	cinema
les magasins (m)	shops
la patinoire	ice rink
la piscine	swimming pool
la plage	beach
le théâtre	theatre
dans	in
derrière	behind
devant	in front of
entre	between

Had a look ☐ **Nearly there** ☐ **Nailed it** ☐

Quand?	When?
aujourd'hui	today
demain	tomorrow
ce/demain matin	this/tomorrow morning
cet/demain après-midi	this/tomorrow afternoon
ce/demain soir	this/tomorrow evening
lundi matin	on Monday morning
samedi soir	on Saturday night

Had a look ☐ **Nearly there** ☐ **Nailed it** ☐

Les amis	Friends
l'ami (m)/le copain	(male) friend
l'amie (f)/la copine	(female) friend
le petit ami/le petit copain	boyfriend

15

Module 1 Vocabulaire

la petite amie/la petite copine	girlfriend
Je retrouve mes amis au parc.	I meet up with my friends in the park.
Je traîne en ville avec mes copines.	I hang out in town with my (female) friends.
Je tchatte en ligne avec ma meilleure copine.	I chat online with my best (female) friend.
Avec mon petit ami, j'écoute de la musique.	I listen to music with my boyfriend.
Je passe chez ma petite copine.	I go to my girlfriend's house.
On rigole bien ensemble.	We have a good laugh together.
On regarde un film ou des clips vidéo.	We watch a film or music videos.
On joue au foot ou au basket ensemble.	We play football or basketball together.
On discute de tout.	We talk about everything.
On mange ensemble au fast-food.	We eat together at a fast-food restaurant.

Had a look ☐   Nearly there ☐   Nailed it ☐

L'amitié / *Friendship*

Je pense que …	I think that …
Pour moi, …	For me …
À mon avis, …	In my opinion …
Un(e) bon(ne) ami(e) est …	A good friend is …
compréhensif/-ive	understanding
cool	cool
drôle	funny
fidèle	loyal
généreux/-euse	generous
gentil(le)	kind
honnête	honest
modeste	modest
optimiste	optimistic
patient(e)	patient
sensible	sensitive
sympa	nice

Had a look ☐   Nearly there ☐   Nailed it ☐

Un(e) bon(ne) ami(e) …	A good friend …
écoute mes problèmes/ mes secrets	listens to my problems/ my secrets
discute de tout avec moi	talks about everything with me
aide tout le monde	helps everyone
accepte mes imperfections	accepts my faults
respecte mes opinions	respects my opinions
a les mêmes centres d'intérêt que moi	has the same interests as me
a le sens de l'humour	has a sense of humour

Had a look ☐   Nearly there ☐   Nailed it ☐

Les rapports de famille / *Family relationships*

French	English
Je m'entends bien avec …	I get on well with …
Je me dispute avec …	I argue with …
Je me chamaille avec …	I bicker with …
Je m'amuse avec …	I have fun with …
Je m'occupe de …	I look after …
le frère aîné/cadet	older/younger brother
la sœur aînée/cadette	older/younger sister
Il/Elle est/a l'air/ semble …	He/She is/looks/ seems …
dynamique	lively
égoïste	selfish
jaloux/-ouse	jealous
sévère	strict
timide	shy
travailleur/-euse	hard-working

Had a look ☐   Nearly there ☐   Nailed it ☐

On va sortir / *Going out*

Je vais …	I am going …
aller à un match	to go to a match
aller au bowling	to go to the bowling alley
aller au cinéma	to go to the cinema
aller à la piscine	to go to the swimming pool
voir un spectacle	to see a show
faire du patin à glace	to go ice-skating
faire du skate	to go skateboarding
faire les magasins	to go shopping
jouer à des jeux vidéo	to play video games
Tu veux venir?	Do you want to come?

Had a look ☐   Nearly there ☐   Nailed it ☐

Les questions / *Questions*

French	English
Quand?	When?
Avec qui?	With who/whom?
On y va comment?	How are we getting there?
On se retrouve où?	Where shall we meet?
On se retrouve à quelle heure?	At what time shall we meet?

Had a look ☐   Nearly there ☐   Nailed it ☐

Une sortie / *An outing*

French	English
J'ai contacté un copain/ une copine.	I contacted a friend.
J'ai quitté la maison.	I left the house.
J'ai raté le bus.	I missed the bus.
Je suis allé(e) en ville.	I went into town.
J'ai écouté de la musique.	I listened to music.
J'ai retrouvé mon copain/ma copine.	I met up with my friend.

Module 1 Vocabulaire

French	English
J'ai discuté avec mon copain/ma copine.	I talked to my friend.
J'ai mangé un sandwich.	I ate a sandwich.
J'ai acheté des vêtements.	I bought some clothes.
C'était super.	It was great.
J'ai passé une très bonne journée.	I had a very good day.

Had a look ☐ **Nearly there** ☐ **Nailed it** ☐

La personne que j'admire / The person I admire

Comment s'appelle la personne que tu admires?	What is the name of the person you admire?
Mon héros s'appelle …	My hero is called …
Mon héroïne s'appelle …	My heroine is called …
Mon modèle s'appelle …	My role model is called …
C'est qui?	Who is he/she?
C'est un pilote de Formule 1.	He is a Formula 1 driver.
C'est un scientifique.	He is a scientist.
C'est une actrice.	She is an actress.
C'est une créatrice de mode.	She is a fashion designer.
Fais-moi sa description physique.	Describe for me what he/she looks like.

Had a look ☐ **Nearly there** ☐ **Nailed it** ☐

French	English
Il/Elle est … petit(e)/gros(se), etc.	He/She is … small/fat, etc.
Il/Elle a les cheveux bruns, etc.	He/She has brown hair, etc.
Quelle est sa personnalité?	What is his/her personality?
Il/Elle est … travailleur/-euse/ créatif/-ive, etc.	He/She is … hard-working/creative, etc.
Pourquoi est-ce que tu admires cette personne?	Why do you admire this person?
J'admire (Stromae/ Malala, etc.) car il/elle …	I admire (Stromae/Malala, etc.) because he/she …
a travaillé très dur	worked/has worked very hard
a joué dans beaucoup de films	acted/has acted in lots of films
a gagné beaucoup de courses	won/has won lots of races
a donné de l'argent à de bonnes œuvres	gave/has given money to good causes
a lutté contre ses problèmes	fought/has fought his/her problems
J'aimerais être comme lui/elle.	I would like to be like him/her.

Had a look ☐ **Nearly there** ☐ **Nailed it** ☐

Module 1 Vocabulaire

Extra words I should know for reading and listening activities

Moi — **Me**
Je suis … — I am …
Je m'appelle …* — I am called …
Je joue le rôle de … — I play the part of …

Had a look ☐ Nearly there ☐ Nailed it ☐

La personne que j'admire — **The person that I admire**
Il/elle a sauvé …** — he/she saved …
Il/elle a aidé …** — he/she helped …
ses vêtements — his/her clothes
ses romans — his/her novels
ses études — his/her studies
son exécution — his/her execution
sa créativité — his/her creativity
sa détermination — his/her determination
un enfant adopté — an adopted child
un(e) auteur(e) — an author

Had a look ☐ Nearly there ☐ Nailed it ☐

un(e) professeur(e) — a teacher
un exemple — an example
un soldat — a soldier
un(e) aviateur/-trice — an aviator
une armée — an army
un camp — a camp
une vie — a life
une université — a university
une maison — a house
une mode — a fashion

Had a look ☐ Nearly there ☐ Nailed it ☐

Comment est ton héros/héroïne? — **What is your hero/heroine like?**
Il/elle est/était … — He/she is/was …
courageux/-euse — brave
de nationalité (pakistanaise) — of (Pakistani) nationality
jeune — young
fort(e) — strong
francophone — French-speaking
mort(e) — dead
vrai(e) — real
algérien(ne) — Algerian

Had a look ☐ Nearly there ☐ Nailed it ☐

Une visite chez … — **A visit to …'s house**
On est invité(e)s à (manger) … — We were invited to (eat) …
On a pris le train tôt/tard. — We got the train early/late.
le matin — in the morning
le soir — in the evening

Had a look ☐ Nearly there ☐ Nailed it ☐

⭐ *Some verbs in French have three parts to them. Without the third part known as the reflexive pronoun, the verb changes its meaning, for example:

Je m'appelle …   I am called …

J'appelle le chien.   I call the dog.

Elle se lève.   She gets up.

Elle lève la chaise.   She lifts up the chair.

⭐ **Past tense actions often end in -é, for example: *Il/elle a aidé* (he/she helped). Without the é, the meaning of the word changes and its sound changes too.

When you read a word with é, or hear this sound, work out the context to find the meaning.

Module 2 Vocabulaire

Words I should know for speaking and writing activities

Les passe-temps — *Hobbies*
Je joue … — *I play …*
au badminton — *badminton*
au basket — *basketball*
au billard — *snooker*
au foot — *football*
au golf — *golf*
au hockey — *hockey*
au rugby — *rugby*
au tennis — *tennis*
au volley — *volleyball*
à la pétanque — *French bowls*
aux cartes (f) — *cards*
aux échecs (m) — *chess*
du piano — *the piano*
du saxophone — *the saxophone*
du violon — *the violin*
de la batterie — *the drums*
de la guitare — *the guitar*
de l'accordéon (m) — *the accordion*
de l'harmonica (m) — *the harmonica*

Had a look ☐ Nearly there ☐ Nailed it ☐

Les expressions de fréquence — *Frequency expressions*
tous les jours — *every day*
tous les soirs — *every evening*
tous les samedis — *every Saturday*
une fois par semaine — *once a week*
deux fois par semaine — *twice a week*
souvent — *often*
de temps en temps — *from time to time*
rarement — *rarely*

Had a look ☐ Nearly there ☐ Nailed it ☐

Les opinions — *Opinions*
Je trouve ça … — *I find that …*
cool/génial — *cool/great*
passionnant/super — *exciting/super*
ennuyeux/nul — *boring/rubbish*
stupide — *stupid*

Had a look ☐ Nearly there ☐ Nailed it ☐

J'aime et je n'aime pas … — *I like and I don't like …*
Ma passion, c'est … — *My passion is …*
le cinéma/le sport/la musique — *the cinema/sport/music*
J'aime/J'adore/Je préfère … — *I like/love/prefer …*
Je n'aime pas/Je déteste … — *I don't like/hate …*

le foot/jouer au foot — *football/playing football*
la lecture/lire — *reading*
la photographie/prendre des photos — *photography/taking photos*

Had a look ☐ Nearly there ☐ Nailed it ☐

Les films — *Films*
une comédie — *a comedy*
un western — *a Western*
un film fantastique — *a fantasy film*
un film d'action — *an action film*
un film d'arts martiaux — *a martial arts film*
un film d'aventure — *an adventure film*
un film d'horreur — *a horror film*
un film de gangsters — *a gangster film*
un film de science-fiction — *a science fiction film*

Had a look ☐ Nearly there ☐ Nailed it ☐

Acheter des billets — *Buying tickets*
Qu'est-ce qu'il y a au cinéma? — *What's on at the cinema?*
La séance commence à quelle heure? — *At what time does the screening start?*
Je peux vous aider? — *Can I help you?*
Je voudrais deux billets pour … — *I would like two tickets for …*
Pour quelle séance? — *For which screening?*
Pour la séance de 19 heures. — *For the screening at 7 p.m.*
Ça coûte combien? — *How much does it cost?*
Le tarif réduit, c'est 14 euros la place. — *The reduced price is 14 euros per seat.*

Had a look ☐ Nearly there ☐ Nailed it ☐

Le sport — *Sport*
Je fais … — *I …*
du footing — *go jogging*
du trampoline — *do trampolining*
du vélo — *go cycling*
de la boxe — *do boxing*
de la danse — *go dancing*
de la natation — *go swimming*
de l'équitation (f) — *go horse-riding*
de l'escalade (f) — *go climbing*
de l'escrime (f) — *do fencing*
des randonnées (f) — *go hiking*
Je fais ça depuis … — *I have been doing that for …*
six mois — *six months*
deux ans — *two years*

Had a look ☐ Nearly there ☐ Nailed it ☐

M 2

19

Module 2 Vocabulaire

Parler de sport / Talking about sport

Français	English
Je préfère les sports individuels.	I prefer individual sports.
Je préfère les sports d'équipe.	I prefer team sports.
Je trouve ça rigolo/facile/rapide	I find it/that fun/easy/fast
Ça me fait du bien.	It does me good.
Ça me détend.	It relaxes me.
Ça booste le moral.	It boosts my/your mood.
C'est bon pour le corps et le mental.	It's good for the body and the mind.
Quand je fais ça, …	When I do/I'm doing it, …
je respire	I breathe
j'oublie mes soucis	I forget my worries

Had a look ☐   Nearly there ☐   Nailed it ☐

Sur mon téléphone portable/ma tablette, … / On my phone/tablet, …

Français	English
je crée des playlists	I create playlists
je télécharge de la musique	I download music
je regarde des clips vidéo	I watch music videos
je joue à des jeux	I play games
je fais des recherches pour mes devoirs	I do research for my homework
je fais des achats	I buy things
j'écris des messages	I write messages
j'écris des articles pour mon blog	I write posts for my blog
je lis mes e-mails	I read my emails
je vais sur des réseaux sociaux	I go onto social media sites
je prends des photos	I take photos
je mets mes photos sur Instagram ou Snapchat	I put my photos on Instagram or Snapchat
À mon avis, c'est …	In my opinion, it's …
génial	great
très pratique	very practical
indispensable	essential

Had a look ☐   Nearly there ☐   Nailed it ☐

Internet / The internet

Français	English
Il est facile de/d' …	It is easy to …
Il est possible de/d' …	It is possible to …
rester en contact avec ses amis	stay in contact with your friends
faire des recherches pour ses devoirs	do research for your homework
utiliser un dico en ligne	use an online dictionary
partager des photos	share photos
Il est dangereux de …	It is dangerous to …
partager ses détails personnels	share your personal details
passer trop de temps sur Internet	spend too much time on the internet
tchatter en ligne avec des inconnus	chat to strangers online
Il est important de …	It is important to …
faire du sport	do some sport
passer du temps avec sa famille	spend some time with your family
retrouver ses amis en vrai	meet up with your friends in real life

Had a look ☐   Nearly there ☐   Nailed it ☐

La lecture / Reading

Français	English
J'apprécie beaucoup les …	I really appreciate/like …
Je préfère les …	I prefer …
J'adore les …	I love …
J'ai une passion pour les …	I'm passionate about …
Je n'aime pas les …	I don't like …
J'ai horreur des …	I hate …
romans fantastiques	fantasy novels
romans policiers	detective novels
romans d'amour	romance novels
livres d'épouvante	horror books
BD	comic books, graphic novels
mangas	mangas
J'aime les illustrations/l'humour.	I like the illustrations/humour.
Je ne lis pas sur une tablette.	I don't read on a tablet.
Je préfère tenir un livre traditionnel dans mes mains.	I prefer holding a traditional book in my hands.
Je ne lis plus de livres traditionnels.	I no longer read traditional books.
Je lis beaucoup en ligne.	I read a lot online.

Had a look ☐   Nearly there ☐   Nailed it ☐

La musique / Music

Français	English
J'aime … /Je n'aime pas …	I like … /I don't like …
le jazz	jazz
le rap	rap
le reggae	reggae
le rock	rock
la musique classique	classical music
la musique pop	pop music
J'écoute ma musique …	I listen to my music …
sur mon téléphone portable avec mes écouteurs.	on my phone with my earphones.
sur mon ordi	on my computer
sur une tablette	on a tablet
Je regarde des clips vidéo pour écouter ma musique.	I watch music videos to listen to my music.

Module 2 Vocabulaire

Mon chanteur préféré/ ma chanteuse préférée, c'est … car … — *My favourite singer is … because …*
j'aime ses paroles — *I like his/her lyrics*
j'aime ses mélodies — *I like his/her tunes*
sa musique me donne envie de danser — *his/her music makes me want to dance*
sa musique me donne envie de chanter — *his/her music makes me want to sing*

Had a look ☐ **Nearly there** ☐ **Nailed it** ☐

Les émissions de télé — *TV programmes*

J'aime/Je n'aime pas … — *I like/I don't like …*
les documentaires (m) — *documentaries*
les jeux télévisés (m) — *game shows*
les magazines culturels (m) — *magazine programmes*
les séries (f) — *series*
les émissions de sport (f) — *sports programmes*
les émissions de musique (f) — *music programmes*
les émissions de télé-réalité (f) — *reality TV programmes*
les actualités (f) — *the news*
parce qu'ils/elles sont … — *because they are/it is …*
amusant(e)s — *funny*
divertissant(e)s — *entertaining*
intéressant(e)s — *interesting*
passionnant(e)s — *exciting*
éducatifs/-ives — *educational*
ennuyeux/-euses — *boring*
(trop) sérieux/-euses — *(too) serious*
originaux/-ales — *original*

Had a look ☐ **Nearly there** ☐ **Nailed it** ☐

Mon émission préférée s'appelle … — *My favourite programme is called …*
C'est un jeu télévisé. — *It's a game show.*
C'est une série. — *It's a drama series.*
J'aime bien l'animateur/-rice. — *I like the presenter.*
Les acteurs sont très doués. — *The actors are very talented.*
Le scénario est passionnant. — *The plot is exciting.*
J'apprends beaucoup. — *I learn a lot.*
Je ne rate jamais cette émission! — *I never miss this programme!*

Had a look ☐ **Nearly there** ☐ **Nailed it** ☐

Une soirée entre amis — *An evening with friends*

Je suis allé(e) au cinéma. — *I went to the cinema.*
Je suis sorti(e) avec … — *I went out with …*
On est allé(e)s à un concert. — *We went to a concert.*
On a vu un film. — *We saw a film.*
On est allé(e)s en ville. — *We went into town.*
On a fait du patin à glace. — *We went ice skating.*
J'ai pris beaucoup de photos. — *I took lots of photos.*
J'ai mis les photos sur Instagram. — *I put the photos on Instagram.*
On est allé(e)s au restaurant. — *We went to a restaurant.*
J'ai bu un coca. — *I drank a cola.*
C'était … — *It was …*
génial — *great*
lamentable — *pathetic*
amusant — *fun, funny*
délicieux — *delicious*

Had a look ☐ **Nearly there** ☐ **Nailed it** ☐

M2

21

Module 2 Vocabulaire

Extra words I should know for reading and listening activities

Tu es sportif/sportive?	Are you sporty?
le marathon de (Paris)	the (Paris) marathon
les sports rapides (m)	quick sports
mon équipe (f)	my team
ensemble	together

Had a look ☐   Nearly there ☐   Nailed it ☐

Ma vie d'internaute	My online life
le blog*	blog
le dico** en ligne	online dictionary
le portable	laptop
la tablette*	tablet
l'ordi** (m)	computer
les réseaux sociaux (m)	social networks
les écouteurs (m)	headphones
apprendre beaucoup de choses	to learn a lot of things
partager des détails personnels avec des inconnus	to share your personal details with strangers
faire des achats	to do shopping
jouer à des jeux	to play games
la photographie	photography

Had a look ☐   Nearly there ☐   Nailed it ☐

Je (ne) lis (pas) …	I (don't) read …
Je trouve …	I find …
Je préfère …	I prefer …
Je pense …	I think …
Je regarde …	I watch …
Je peux …	I can …
J'adore …	I love …
J'aime (bien) …	I (really) like …
J'apprécie …	I appreciate …
J'écoute …	I listen …

Had a look ☐   Nearly there ☐   Nailed it ☐

*Lots of new technology-related words are the same in French as in English, for example: *le blog, la tablette*.

**Remember that you can abbreviate words in French too, for example: *ordi* (*ordinateur*), *dico* (*dictionnaire*). So, if you encounter a word that you don't recognise, think about whether it is a shorter version of a word that you already know. The context that the word is in will help you to do this.

Module 3 Vocabulaire

Words I should know for speaking and writing activities

La nourriture et les boissons	Food and drink
du beurre	butter
du fromage	cheese
du lait	milk
du pain	bread
du poisson	fish
du poulet	chicken
du yaourt	yoghurt
de la confiture	jam
de la glace	ice cream
de la viande	meat
de l'eau (f)	water
des bananes (f)	bananas
des fraises (f)	strawberries
des œufs (m)	eggs
des pêches (f)	peaches
des poires (f)	pears
des pommes (f)	apples
des pommes de terre (f)	potatoes

Had a look ☐ Nearly there ☐ Nailed it ☐

Les repas	Meals
Qu'est-ce que tu prends pour le petit-déjeuner?	What do you have for breakfast?
Qu'est-ce que tu manges à midi?	What do you eat at lunchtime?
Qu'est-ce que tu manges comme casse-croûte?	What do you have as a snack?
Qu'est-ce que tu manges, le soir?	What do you eat in the evening?
Qu'est-ce que tu bois?	What do you drink?
Pour le petit-déjeuner, ...	For breakfast, ...
À midi, ...	At lunchtime, ...
Comme casse-croûte, ...	As a snack, ...
Le soir, ...	In the evening, ...
Comme dessert, ...	For dessert, ...
Je prends/Je mange ...	I have/I eat ...
des céréales (f)	cereal
du pain grillé	toast
un sandwich	a sandwich
des chips (f)	crisps
des biscuits (m)	biscuits
des pâtes (f)	pasta
de la salade	salad
de la glace au chocolat	chocolate ice cream
Je bois du jus d'orange.	I drink orange juice.

Had a look ☐ Nearly there ☐ Nailed it ☐

Les quantités	Quantities
un kilo de ...	a kilo of ...
deux cent cinquante grammes de ...	250 grams of ...
un litre de ...	a litre of ...
un paquet de ...	a packet of ...
un pot de ...	a jar/pot of ...
une boîte de ...	a tin/can of ...
une bouteille de ...	a bottle of ...
quatre tranches de ...	four slices of ...

Had a look ☐ Nearly there ☐ Nailed it ☐

Les vêtements	Clothes
Je porte ...	I wear/am wearing ...
un blouson	a jacket
un chapeau	a hat
un costume	a suit
un imperméable	a raincoat
un jean (moulant)	(a pair of) (skinny) jeans
un manteau	a coat
un pantalon	(a pair of) trousers
un polo	a polo shirt
un pull	a jumper
un sac à main	a handbag
un short	(a pair of) shorts
un sweat à capuche	a hoody
un tee-shirt	a T-shirt
une casquette	a cap
une ceinture	a belt

Had a look ☐ Nearly there ☐ Nailed it ☐

une chemise	a shirt
une écharpe	a scarf
une mini-jupe	a miniskirt
une montre	a watch
une robe	a dress
une veste	a jacket
des baskets (de marque) (f)	(designer) trainers
des boucles d'oreille (f)	earrings
des bottes (f)	boots
des chaussettes (f)	socks
des chaussures (f)	shoes
des gants (m)	gloves
des lunettes de soleil (f)	sunglasses
en laine	woollen
en cuir	leather
rayé(e)(s)	striped

Had a look ☐ Nearly there ☐ Nailed it ☐

Les couleurs	Colours
blanc(he)(s)	white
bleu(e)(s)	blue
gris(e)(s)	grey
jaune(s)	yellow
marron	brown

Module 3 Vocabulaire

mauve(s)	purple
noir(e)(s)	black
orange	orange
rose(s)	pink
rouge(s)	red
vert(e)(s)	green
clair	light
foncé	dark
multicolore(s)	multi-coloured

Had a look ☐ Nearly there ☐ Nailed it ☐

La vie quotidienne — Daily life

J'ai cours tous les jours sauf …	I have lessons every day except …
Les jours d'école, …	On school days …
je dois me lever tôt	I have to get up early
je dois quitter la maison à (7h30)	I have to leave the house at (7:30 a.m.)
Le soir, …	In the evening, …
je dois faire mes devoirs	I have to do my homework
je dois aider ma mère	I have to help my mother
je peux regarder un peu la télé	I can watch a bit of TV
Le samedi, …	On Saturdays, …
Le dimanche, …	On Sundays, …
je peux rester au lit	I can stay in bed
je peux retrouver mes copains/copines en ville	I can meet up with my friends in town
je dois ranger ma chambre	I have to tidy my room
je peux écouter de la musique	I can listen to music

Had a look ☐ Nearly there ☐ Nailed it ☐

Au magasin de vêtements — In the clothes shop

la taille	size
la pointure	shoe size
les cabines d'essayage (f)	changing rooms
une taille moyenne	medium size
Il y a un trou.	There's a hole (in it).
Il y a une tache.	There's a stain (on it).
Il/Elle est … /Ils/Elles sont …	It is … /They are …
trop petit(e)(s)	too small
trop grand(e)(s)	too big
cassé(e)(s)	broken
Il/Elle ne marche pas.	It is not working/doesn't work.
Je voudrais …	I would like …
échanger (la jupe/le pantalon, etc.)	to exchange (the skirt/trousers, etc.)
un remboursement	a refund

Had a look ☐ Nearly there ☐ Nailed it ☐

Faire les magasins ou faire du shopping en ligne? — Go to the shops or shop online?

Je préfère …	I prefer …
faire les magasins	to go to the shops
faire mes achats en ligne	to make my purchases online
parce que/qu' …	because …
c'est mieux d'essayer les vêtements dans un magasin	it's better to try clothes on in a shop
je peux demander l'opinion de mes ami(e)s	I can ask my friends' opinion
il y a trop de monde dans les magasins	there are too many people in the shops
on peut trouver des vêtements moins chers	you can find cheaper clothes
c'est plus facile/plus rapide	it's easier/faster

Had a look ☐ Nearly there ☐ Nailed it ☐

Les fêtes — Festivals

Noël	Christmas
la veille de Noël	Christmas Eve
Pâques	Easter
Divali	Diwali
Hanoukka	Hanukkah
Aïd-el-Fitr	Eid al-Fitr
le 6 janvier/la fête des Rois	Epiphany
le premier avril	April Fool's Day
la Chandeleur	Candlemas
le Nouvel An	New Year
la Saint-Sylvestre	New Year's Eve
la Saint-Valentin	Valentine's Day
la fête des Mères	Mother's Day
le 14 juillet/la fête nationale française	Bastille Day, 14 July
On est chrétiens.	We are Christian.
On est juifs.	We are Jewish.
On est musulmans.	We are Muslim.

Had a look ☐ Nearly there ☐ Nailed it ☐

Chez moi/nous …	At my/our house …
on fête (Noël/Divali, etc.)	we celebrate (Christmas/Diwali, etc.)
on boit du champagne	we drink champagne
on décore le sapin de Noël	we decorate the Christmas tree
on s'offre des cadeaux	we give each other presents
on ouvre les cadeaux	we open the presents
on chante des chants traditionnels	we sing traditional songs
on allume des bougies	we light candles

24

Module 3 Vocabulaire

on cherche des œufs dans le jardin — we look for eggs in the garden
On prépare/mange ... — We prepare/eat ...
de la dinde rôtie — roast turkey
des légumes (m) — vegetables
une bûche de Noël au chocolat — a chocolate Yule log
des crêpes (f) — crêpes
une galette des Rois — tart eaten for Epiphany
toutes sortes de bonnes choses — all sorts of good things
des choses sucrées — sweet things

Had a look ☐ Nearly there ☐ Nailed it ☐

Un repas spécial — A special meal
Je vais/On va apporter ... — I am/We are going to bring ...
du jambon — ham
du pâté — pâté
du saucisson — salami
des baguettes (f) — baguettes
des biftecks (m) — steaks
des saucisses (f) — sausages
des salades composées (f) — mixed salads
une salade de riz — a rice salad
du concombre — cucumber
une laitue — a lettuce
des tomates (f) — tomatoes
des oignons (m) — onions
des poivrons (m) — peppers
des champignons (m) — mushrooms
des abricots (m) — apricots
des framboises (f) — raspberries
du raisin — grapes
des mini-gâteaux (m) — mini-cakes
une tarte aux fruits — a fruit tart

Had a look ☐ Nearly there ☐ Nailed it ☐

Les magasins — Shops
le marché — market
le supermarché — supermarket
la boucherie — butcher's
la boulangerie — bakery, baker's
la charcuterie — pork butcher's, delicatessen
la pâtisserie — cake shop, pastry shop
l'épicerie (f) — greengrocer's

Had a look ☐ Nearly there ☐ Nailed it ☐

Fêter le 14 juillet — Celebrating Bastille Day
On va aller au bal. — We're going to go to the dance.
On va regarder le feu d'artifice. — We're going to watch the fireworks.
On va s'amuser. — We're going to have fun.
On va inviter ... — We're going to invite ...

Had a look ☐ Nearly there ☐ Nailed it ☐

Félicitations! — Congratulations!
l'anniversaire (m) — birthday
le mariage — wedding, marriage
la fête — party
C'était mon anniversaire. — It was my birthday.
J'ai reçu beaucoup de cadeaux. — I received lots of presents.
Ma sœur a eu son premier bébé. — My sister had her first baby.
Je suis allé(e) au mariage de (ma cousine). — I went to (my cousin's) wedding.
Mon frère s'est pacsé avec son compagnon. — My brother entered into a civil partnership with his partner.
Il y avait ... — There was/were ...
beaucoup d'invités — lots of guests
un gâteau spécial — a special cake
C'était ... — It was ...
génial — great

Had a look ☐ Nearly there ☐ Nailed it ☐

M3

25

Module 3 Vocabulaire

Extra words I should know for reading and listening activities

On fait du shopping!
Ça me déstresse!*
Vous désirez?
Avez-vous … ?
Ça fait combien?
Je prends …
Je suis désolé(e) …
Je n'en ai plus.
Alors …
Bien sûr.
Ça fait (huit) euros, s'il vous plaît.

Let's go shopping!
It de-stresses me!
How can I help you?
Have you got … ?
How much is that?
I'll have …
I'm sorry …
I haven't got any more.
Well/So …
Of course.
That's (eight) euros, please.

Had a look ☐ Nearly there ☐ Nailed it ☐

Les fêtes en France
On colle un poisson dans le dos de quelqu'un.**
On dit («Poisson d'avril!»).**
On mange …
Comme dessert …
J'adore/J'aime fêter mon anniversaire.
Je reçois beaucoup de cadeaux.
À part (Noël) …
Je suis né(e) (en août).
Le jour de (mon anniversaire) …
C'est l'occasion de dire merci à (sa maman).
Je suis (très) romantique.
Une de mes fêtes préférées, c'est …
J'aime m'habiller bien.
le compte à rebours
Tout le monde s'embrasse.*

Festivals/Parties in France
We stick a fish onto someone's back.

We say ("April Fool's Day!").
We eat …
As a dessert …
I love/like celebrating my birthday.
I get lots of presents.
Apart from (Christmas) …
I was born (in August).
The day of (my birthday) …
It's the time to say thank you to (your mum).
I am (very) romantic.
One of my favourite festivals is …
I like to dress well.
the countdown
Everyone kisses each other.

Had a look ☐ Nearly there ☐ Nailed it ☐

Un repas spécial
Je vais m'occuper (du dessert).
Je viens!
Je vais chercher (le pain).
Je vais faire cuire (des morceaux de poulet).
Compte sur nous!
On va préparer/boire …

On va acheter à boire!

Des (grandes) bouteilles de …
On mange chez mes grands-parents/nous.
Cette année/fois …
Je vais inviter toute ma famille (à un barbecue).
La ville où on habite …
Je (ne) peux (pas) aller au supermarché.
Je dois acheter les provisions dans des magasins indépendants.
Avec ça, je vais servir …

A special meal
I'll take care of (the dessert).
I'm coming!
I'm going to get (the bread).
I'm going to cook (chicken pieces).
Count on us!
We are going to prepare/drink …
We are going to buy the drinks.
(Big) bottles of …

We eat at my grandparents' house/our house.
This year/time …
I'm going to invite all of my family (to a barbecue).
The town where we live …
I can('t) go to the supermarket.
I have to get the food from small/independent shops.
I'm going to serve … with that.

Had a look ☐ Nearly there ☐ Nailed it ☐

Félicitations!
Il y avait beaucoup d'invités.
J'ai pris des photos.
la cérémonie
le vin d'honneur
un croquembouche**

J'ai fêté …
C'était une (excellente) soirée!

Congratulations!
There were lots of people invited.
I took some photos.
the ceremony
drinks reception
special (wedding) cake, made of profiteroles and cream
I celebrated …
It was a (great) night!

Had a look ☐ Nearly there ☐ Nailed it ☐

 *Use cognates/near cognates to work out new words and phrases such as *Ça me déstresse!* or *Tout le monde s'embrasse!*

**Some French customs are different to English ones, such as the cake served at weddings. Make a list in French and English and learn them.

Module 4 Vocabulaire

Words I should know for speaking and writing activities

Où habites-tu?
Where do you live?
J'habite … | I live …
dans une ville/un village | in a town/village
au centre-ville | in the town centre
au bord de la mer | at the seaside
à la campagne/montagne | in the countryside/mountains
en ville | in town
à Londres/Manchester, etc. | in London/Manchester, etc.
dans le nord/le sud/l'est/l'ouest … | in the north/south/east/west …
dans le centre … | in the centre …
de l'Angleterre/Écosse/Irlande (du Nord) | of England/Scotland/(Northern) Ireland
de la France | of France
du pays de Galles | of Wales

Had a look ☐ Nearly there ☐ Nailed it ☐

Qu'est-ce qu'on peut faire?
What can you do?
On peut … | You can …
aller à un match de foot | go to a football match
aller au cinéma | go to the cinema
faire du cheval | go horse-riding
faire du ski | go skiing
faire du snowboard | go snowboarding
faire des promenades | go for walks
faire les magasins | go shopping
se baigner dans la mer | swim/bathe in the sea
se détendre sur la plage | relax on the beach
visiter le château | visit the castle
visiter les musées | visit the museums

Had a look ☐ Nearly there ☐ Nailed it ☐

Dans ma ville/mon village
In my town/village
Dans ma ville/mon village, il y a … | In my town/village, there is/are …
un bureau de poste/une poste | a post office
un centre de loisirs | a leisure centre
un château | a castle
un marché | a market
un musée | a museum
un parc/jardin public | a park
un stade | a stadium
un supermarché | a supermarket
une bibliothèque | a library
une église | a church
une gare (SNCF) | a (railway) station
une mosquée | a mosque
des hôtels (m) | some hotels
des restaurants (m) | some restaurants
Il n'y a pas de … | There isn't a/aren't any …

Had a look ☐ Nearly there ☐ Nailed it ☐

Les directions
Directions
Où est le/la/l' … ? | Where is the … ?
Où sont les … ? | Where are the … ?
Pour aller au/à la/à l'/aux … ? | How do I get to the … ?
Va/Allez tout droit. | Go straight on.
Tourne/Tournez à gauche/droite. | Turn left/right.
Prends/Prenez la première/deuxième/troisième rue à gauche/droite. | Take the first/second/third street on the left/right.
Traverse/Traversez le pont/la place. | Cross the bridge/square.
Descends/Descendez la rue. | Go down the street.
C'est près/loin? | Is it near/far?
C'est tout près/assez loin. | It's very near/quite far.

Had a look ☐ Nearly there ☐ Nailed it ☐

Qu'est-ce qu'il y a dans ta région?
What is there in your region?
Dans ma région, il y a … | In my region there is/are …
un lac | a lake
un port de pêche | a fishing port
une rivière/un fleuve | a river
des champs (m) | fields
des collines (f) | hills
des fermes (f) | farms
des forêts (f) | forests
des stations de ski (f) | ski resorts
des vignobles (m) | vineyards
En Bretagne, il y a … | In Brittany there is/are …
un beau château | a beautiful castle
une belle cathédrale | a beautiful cathedral
des villes historiques | historical towns
de vieilles maisons | old houses
de vieux bâtiments | old buildings
On peut … | You can …
faire de la voile | go sailing
faire des randonnées à vélo | go for bike rides

Had a look ☐ Nearly there ☐ Nailed it ☐

Le meilleur …
The best …
le meilleur climat | the best climate
la meilleure équipe de football | the best football team

M 4

27

Module 4 Vocabulaire

le plus beau paysage	the most beautiful countryside	Avez-vous un dépliant/ un plan de la ville?	Do you have a leaflet/a map of the town?
les plus belles plages	the most beautiful beaches	Où est-ce qu'on peut acheter des billets?	Where can we buy tickets?
le plus long fleuve	the longest river	la durée	duration
la plus longue piste de ski	the longest ski slope	les tarifs (m)	prices
		gratuit(e)	free
la plus haute tour	the highest tower	accessible aux personnes handicapées	accessible to disabled people
le musée le plus populaire	the most popular museum	les chiens sont acceptés	dogs are welcome
la région la plus historique	the most historical region	Had a look ☐ Nearly there ☐ Nailed it ☐	
les stations de ski (f) les plus populaires	the most popular ski resorts	**Le temps/La météo**	***The weather/The weather forecast***
les monuments (m) les plus célèbres	the most famous monuments	Quel temps fait-il?	What is the weather like?
Had a look ☐ Nearly there ☐ Nailed it ☐		Il fait beau.	The weather is good.
		Il fait mauvais.	The weather is bad.
		Il fait chaud.	It's hot.
Visiter une ville	***Visiting a town***	Il fait froid.	It's cold.
Je voudrais visiter/ voir …	*I would like to visit/see …*	Il y a du soleil.	It's sunny.
		Il y a du brouillard.	It's foggy.
Je ne voudrais pas rater …	*I wouldn't want to miss …*	Il y a du vent.	It's windy.
		Il y a un orage.	There's a storm.
l'aquarium (m)	*the aquarium*	Il pleut.	It's raining.
l'exposition (f) sur …	*the exhibition on …*	Il neige.	It's snowing.
le spectacle son et lumière	*the sound and light show*	près de la Manche	near the Channel
		sur la côte atlantique	on the Atlantic coast
Je voudrais louer des vélos.	*I would like to hire bikes.*	sur la côte méditerranéenne	on the Mediterranean coast
J'aimerais …	*I would like …*	Had a look ☐ Nearly there ☐ Nailed it ☐	
faire une promenade en bateau	*to go on a boat trip*		
monter à la tour de l'horloge	*to climb the clock tower*	**Les projets**	***Plans***
		aujourd'hui	today
Had a look ☐ Nearly there ☐ Nailed it ☐		demain	tomorrow
		après-demain	the day after tomorrow
		ce week-end	this weekend
		cette semaine	this week
		S'il fait beau/mauvais (etc.), on va …	If the weather's good/bad (etc.), we're going …
Les renseignements touristiques	***Tourist information***	aller à la pêche	to go fishing
(Le château) est ouvert quels jours de la semaine?	*On what days is (the castle) open?*	aller à la piscine (en plein air)	to go to the (open-air) swimming pool
		faire un barbecue	to have a barbecue
C'est ouvert (tous les jours/tous les jours sauf le dimanche).	*It's open (every day/every day except Sundays).*	faire un pique-nique	to have a picnic
		faire de la luge	to go tobogganing
		rester à la maison	to stay at home
Quels sont les horaires d'ouverture?	*What are the opening hours?*	regarder la télé	to watch TV
C'est ouvert de (9h) à (17h).	*It's open from (9 a.m.) until (5 p.m.).*	Had a look ☐ Nearly there ☐ Nailed it ☐	
C'est combien, l'entrée?	*How much is the entrance fee?*	**Ville de rêve ou ville de cauchemar?**	***Dream town or nightmare town?***
Ça coûte … pour les adultes et … pour les enfants.	*It costs … for adults and … for children.*	C'est …	It's …
		très animé	very lively
Est-ce qu'il y a un restaurant ou une cafétéria?	*Is there a restaurant or a cafeteria?*	trop tranquille	too quiet

28

Module 4 Vocabulaire

sale	*dirty*
pollué(e)	*polluted*
triste	*sad*
Ce n'est jamais propre.	*It's never clean.*
Il y a …	*There is/are …*
de bons transports en commun	*good public transport*
seulement des maisons et une église	*only houses and a church*
trop de circulation	*too much traffic*
trop de bruit	*too much noise*
toujours des déchets par terre	*always rubbish on the ground*
Il n'y a rien pour les jeunes.	*There is nothing for young people.*
Il n'y a pas grand-chose à faire.	*There is not much to do.*
Il n'y a pas de zone piétonne.	*There is no pedestrian precinct.*
Il n'y a plus de cinéma.	*There is no longer a cinema.*
Le cinéma est fermé.	*The cinema is closed (down).*
un club pour les jeunes	*a youth club*
les poubelles (f)	*bins*
en banlieue	*in the suburbs*
le quartier	*neighbourhood, district, part of town*

Had a look ☐   **Nearly there** ☐   **Nailed it** ☐

M 4

29

Module 4 Vocabulaire

Extra words I should know for reading and listening activities

Qu'est-ce qu'il y a où tu habites?
What is there where you live?

des belles plages	beautiful beaches
des beaux châteaux	beautiful castles
des grandes forêts	large forests
la capitale	the capital
la plus haute montagne de France*	the highest mountain in France
le plus grand château de France et du monde*	The biggest castle in France and the world
la meilleure équipe de foot*	The best football team

Had a look ☐ **Nearly there** ☐ **Nailed it** ☐

Les renseignements touristiques
Tourist information

Ça, c'est plus intéressant!	That's more interesting!
le spectacle son et lumière	sound and lights show
une promenade (commentée) en bateau	(guided) boat trip
une randonnée à vélo	bike ride
les requins (m)	sharks
les navettes spatiales (f)	space shuttles
environ	about
l'horloge (f)	clock tower

Had a look ☐ **Nearly there** ☐ **Nailed it** ☐

Les activités
Activities

dans le jardin	in the garden
pendant les vacances	during the holidays

Had a look ☐ **Nearly there** ☐ **Nailed it** ☐

C'est comment où tu habites?
What is it like where you live?

tout** ...	very ...
... petit	... small
... propre	... clean
... triste	... sad
culturel(le)	cultural
mon quartier	my neighbourhood
Il (n')y a ... (rien) pour les jeunes.	There is ... (nothing) for young people.
Il y avait ...	There used to be ...
un endroit sans pollution	a place without pollution
complètement	completely
J'ai repondu à un sondage en ligne.	I answered an online survey.
les aspects de la ville	the aspects of the town
Il faut avoir ...	You should have ...
Je veux habiter (dans) un endroit propre.	I want to live in a clean place.

Had a look ☐ **Nearly there** ☐ **Nailed it** ☐

⭐ *Learn key geographical, cultural or historical aspects about France, such as which is the longest river, the highest mountain, etc. You can use them in the speaking exam to impress the examiner. This knowledge will also help you understand more easily passages in the reading and listening exams.

⭐ **Be very careful of words that can have more than one meaning. *Tout* can mean 'all', 'quite', 'every', 'any' and 'very'!

Another example is *de*, which depending on the context means 'from', 'of', 'some' and 'in'.

Module 5 Vocabulaire

Words I should know for speaking and writing activities

Les pays	**Countries**
le Danemark	Denmark
le Pakistan	Pakistan
le pays de Galles	Wales
le Royaume-Uni	the UK
l'Algérie (f)	Algeria
l'Allemagne (f)	Germany
l'Angleterre (f)	England
l'Autriche (f)	Austria
la Belgique	Belgium
l'Espagne (f)	Spain
l'Italie (f)	Italy
la Pologne	Poland
la Russie	Russia
la Suisse	Switzerland
les États-Unis (m)	the USA
les Pays-Bas (m)	the Netherlands

Had a look ☐ **Nearly there** ☐ **Nailed it** ☐

Les vacances	**Holidays**
Où vas-tu en vacances?	Where do you go on holiday?
Je vais …	I go …
en France	to France
au pays de Galles	to Wales
aux États-Unis	to the USA
Comment voyages-tu?	How do you travel?
Je voyage …	I travel …
en avion	by plane
en bateau	by boat
en car	by coach
en train	by train
en voiture	by car
à vélo	by bike
Où loges-tu?	Where do you stay?
Je loge dans …	I stay in/on …
un camping	a campsite
un hôtel	a hotel
une auberge de jeunesse	a youth hostel
une caravane	a caravan

Had a look ☐ **Nearly there** ☐ **Nailed it** ☐

Avec qui pars-tu en vacances?	Who do you go on holiday with?
Je pars …	I go …
avec ma famille	with my family
avec mes copains/copines	with my friends
avec mes grands-parents	with my grandparents
seul(e)	alone
C'est comment?	What's it like?
C'est …	It's …
extra/formidable	amazing/great
bien	good
ennuyeux/nul	boring/rubbish
Ce n'est pas mal.	It's not bad.

Had a look ☐ **Nearly there** ☐ **Nailed it** ☐

Les hôtels	**Hotels**
un hôtel	a hotel
des chambres d'hôtes	guest rooms (i.e. in a B&B/guest house)
Nous proposons des chambres avec …	We offer rooms with …
un grand lit	a double bed
un lit simple	a single bed
une salle de bains	a bathroom
une douche	a shower
un micro-ondes	a microwave
une télévision à écran plat	a flat-screen TV
(une) vue sur la mer	a sea view
un balcon	a balcony
la climatisation	air conditioning

Had a look ☐ **Nearly there** ☐ **Nailed it** ☐

Nous avons aussi …	We also have …
une aire de jeux	a games area
un parking	a car park
une piscine	a swimming pool
un restaurant	a restaurant
le Wi-Fi	Wi-Fi
Nos chambres sont bien équipées.	Our rooms are well equipped.
Le petit-déjeuner est inclus/compris.	Breakfast is included.
Notre hôtel est situé/se trouve …	Our hotel is located …

Had a look ☐ **Nearly there** ☐ **Nailed it** ☐

Réserver une chambre	**Booking a room**
Nous voulons/Je voudrais réserver une chambre …	We want/I would like to book a room …
pour une/deux personne(s)	for one person/two people
avec un lit simple/un grand lit	with a single/double bed
pour une nuit/deux nuits	for one night/two nights
Est-ce que vous avez … ?	Do you have … ?
une piscine	a swimming pool
la climatisation	air conditioning
Votre chambre est …	Your room is …

31

Module 5 Vocabulaire

au rez-de-chaussée	on the ground floor	moins ennuyeux/fatigant	less boring/tiring
au premier étage	on the first floor	moins cher	less expensive
au deuxième étage	on the second floor		
Je voudrais payer avec ma carte bancaire.	I would like to pay with my debit/credit card.	Had a look ☐ Nearly there ☐ Nailed it ☐	

Had a look ☐ Nearly there ☐ Nailed it ☐

Voyager / Travelling

l'aéroport (m)	airport
le billet	ticket
le conducteur/la conductrice	driver
le contrôle des passeports	passport control
le guichet	ticket office/counter
le/la pilote	pilot
le quai	platform
l'autoroute (f)	motorway
la ceinture de sécurité	seatbelt
la circulation	traffic
la douane	customs
la gare	station
la route	road
les bagages (m)	luggage

Les activités en vacances / Holiday activities

Je fais de la planche à voile.	I go windsurfing.
Je fais de la voile.	I go sailing.
Je fais de l'accrobranche.	I do a tree-top adventure.
Je fais du ski.	I go skiing.
Je visite les musées.	I visit the museums.
Je visite les monuments.	I visit the monuments.
Je vais à la pêche.	I go fishing.
Je vais à la plage.	I go to the beach.
Je joue à la pétanque.	I play French bowls.
Je me baigne.	I swim (in the sea).
Je me promène.	I go for a walk.
Je me repose.	I rest.
Je me lève (tôt/tard).	I get up (early/late).
Je m'habille.	I get dressed.
Je ne m'ennuie pas.	I don't get bored.
Je sors au restaurant.	I go out to a restaurant.

Had a look ☐ Nearly there ☐ Nailed it ☐

Had a look ☐ Nearly there ☐ Nailed it ☐

Au guichet / At the ticket counter

Je peux vous aider?	Can I help you?
Je voudrais un aller simple/un aller-retour pour (Lyon), s'il vous plaît.	I would like a single/a return to (Lyon), please.
En quelle classe?	In which class?
En première/deuxième classe.	In first/second class.
C'est quel quai?	Which platform is it?
Le train part à quelle heure?	What time does the train leave?
Le voyage dure combien de temps?	How long does the journey last?
Est-ce qu'il faut changer?	Do I/we have to change?
C'est un train direct.	The train is direct.

Au restaurant / At the restaurant

Voici la carte.	Here is the menu.
Le plat du jour, c'est …	The daily special is …
Vous avez fait votre choix?	Have you made your choice?
Pour commencer, je vais prendre …	To start, I am going to have …
Comme plat principal, je voudrais …	As a main course, I would like …
Je vais prendre le menu (à 30 euros).	I am going to have the (30 euro) set menu.
Et comme boisson?	And to drink?
Qu'est-ce que vous avez comme desserts?	What desserts do you have?
Vous avez besoin d'autre chose?	Do you need anything else?
On a besoin de l'addition.	We need the bill.
J'ai faim.	I am hungry.
J'ai soif.	I am thirsty.
J'ai envie d'un dessert.	I want a dessert.

Had a look ☐ Nearly there ☐ Nailed it ☐

Had a look ☐ Nearly there ☐ Nailed it ☐

Moyens de transports préférés et raisons / Favourite means of transport and reasons

Je voyage toujours (en train, etc.) parce que c'est …	I always travel (by train, etc.) because it's …
plus rapide/plus confortable	faster/more comfortable
plus pratique/plus vert	more practical/greener
plus aventureux	more adventurous
mieux/meilleur pour la planète	better for the planet

Les plats / Dishes

les entrées (f)	starters
les brochettes (f) de crevettes (f)	prawn skewers
les escargots (m)	snails
la soupe à la tomate	tomato soup

Module 5 Vocabulaire

la tarte à l'oignon	onion tart	**Des vacances catastrophiques**	**Catastrophic holidays**
les plats principaux (m)	main dishes	J'ai oublié mon passeport.	I forgot my passport.
l'épaule d'agneau (f)	shoulder of lamb	J'ai pris un coup de soleil.	I got sunburnt.
la cuisse de canard	duck leg		
les lasagnes végétariennes (f)	vegetarian lasagne	J'ai cassé mon appareil photo.	I broke my camera.
le loup de mer	sea bass	J'ai été malade.	I got sick.
le poulet basquaise	Basque-style chicken	On m'a volé mon sac.	Someone stole my handbag.
le rôti de veau	roast veal		
les desserts (m)	desserts	Il a plu tous les jours.	It rained every day.
la crème brûlée	crème brûlée	Il y avait des cafards dans notre chambre.	There were cockroaches in our room.
la mousse au chocolat	chocolate mousse		
le roulé au chocolat	chocolate roll	J'ai raté l'avion.	I missed the plane.
le sorbet	sorbet	J'ai dû aller chez le médecin.	I had to go to the doctor.
la tarte au citron	lemon tart		
la tarte aux pommes	apple tart	J'ai perdu mes photos.	I lost my photos.
l'eau gazeuse (f)	sparkling water	J'ai vomi.	I vomited.

Had a look ☐ **Nearly there** ☐ **Nailed it** ☐

J'ai dû aller au commissariat. — I had to go to the police station.

Critiques / Reviews

J'y suis allé(e) pour le déjeuner/le dîner.	I went there for lunch/dinner.
Le service était lent/exceptionnel.	The service was slow/exceptional.
Le serveur/La serveuse était/n'était pas (très) poli(e).	The waiter/waitress was/wasn't (very) polite.
C'était … délicieux/bien cuit.	It was … delicious/well-cooked.
La nourriture était froide/trop salée.	The food was cold/too salty.
La nourriture n'était pas cuite.	The food wasn't cooked.
Je recommande/Je ne recommande pas ce restaurant.	I recommend/don't recommend this restaurant.

Il n'y avait rien à faire. — There was nothing to do.
On a dû chercher un autre hôtel. — We had to look for another hotel.
La prochaine fois, je vais … — Next time, I am going …
faire plus attention — to be more careful
mettre de la crème solaire — to put on sun cream
loger dans un camping — to stay on a campsite

Had a look ☐ **Nearly there** ☐ **Nailed it** ☐

Had a look ☐ **Nearly there** ☐ **Nailed it** ☐

M5

33

Module 5 Vocabulaire

Extra words I should know for reading and listening activities

L'hébergement / Accommodation
un hôtel familial/de luxe	a family/luxury hotel by the river
au bord du fleuve	
un hôtel 4 étoiles prêt à vous accueillir	a four-star hotel ready to welcome you
spacieux/-euse(s)	spacious
notre maison	our house
au premier/deuxième étage	on the first/second floor
un parking à votre disposition	a car park for you
tout de suite	straightaway
une salle de bains privée	a private bathroom
une piscine extérieure	an outdoor swimming pool
toutes les formules possibles	all possible options
une aire de jeux	a play area
confortable/parfait	comfortable/perfect
Nous mettons …	We put …
Nous proposons …	We offer …
Nous avons une chambre pour … personnes(s).	We have a room for … people.
bien situé(e)	well-situated
dormir	to sleep
ouvert(e)/fermé(e) toute l'année	open/closed all year

Had a look ☐ Nearly there ☐ Nailed it ☐

Pour réserver un hôtel / To reserve a hotel
(Comment) voulez-vous (payer)?	(How) do you want (to pay)?
Quelle sorte de … ?	What type of … ?
Combien de nuits?	How many nights?

Had a look ☐ Nearly there ☐ Nailed it ☐

En route! / On the road!
(Le train) arrive à quelle heure?	What time does (the train) arrive?
Bon voyage!	Have a good trip!
Je vais (aller) …*	I go/am going (to go) …
J'y vais …	I go there …
J'aime (beaucoup) … prendre l'avion	I (really) like … to take the plane
(y) aller en ferry	to go by ferry
rencontrer des gens	to meet people
voyager en voiture	to travel by car
faire du vélo	to go cycling
C'est tout simplement la classe!	It's simply awesome!
Quand y vas-tu?	When do you go?
tous les ans	every year
le lendemain	the day after tomorrow
C'est (nettement) mieux.	It's (clearly) better.
en (juillet)	in (July)
Que fais-tu?	What do you do?

Had a look ☐ Nearly there ☐ Nailed it ☐

Les vacances de l'année dernière / Last year's holidays
C'était mon premier/dernier jour de vacances.	It was my first/last day of the holidays.
J'ai décidé de …	I decided to …
Je me suis levé(e) …	I got up …
très tôt	very early
tard	late
à midi	at midday
Je suis allé(e) …	I went …
à la plage	to the beach
en boîte	to a nightclub
J'ai retrouvé des amis …	I met friends …
J'ai vu le lever du soleil.	I saw the sunrise.
J'ai dansé au soleil/sous le soleil.	I danced in the sun.
Qu'est-ce que c'était beau!	How beautiful it was!

Had a look ☐ Nearly there ☐ Nailed it ☐

Bon appétit! / Enjoy your food!
Pour commencer, je vais prendre …	To start, I am going to have …
Pour moi …	For me …
J'ai (très) faim.	I'm (very) hungry.
Vous avez besoin d'autre chose?	Would you like anything else?
L'addition, s'il vous plaît.	The bill, please.
C'était froid/parfait/délicieux.	It was cold/perfect/delicious.

Had a look ☐ Nearly there ☐ Nailed it ☐

Les catastrophes! / Catastrophes!
Quel dommage!	What a shame!
J'ai passé une nuit dans un hôtel sale.	I spent a night in a dirty hotel.
Il y avait une odeur bizarre.	There was a strange smell.
La salle de bains n'était pas propre non plus!	The bathroom wasn't clean either!
La climatisation était cassée.	The air conditionning was broken.

Had a look ☐ Nearly there ☐ Nailed it ☐

> ⭐ *Je fais … and Je vais … can both be translated as 'I go …'. However, you can only use Je vais … to mean 'I go …' with a destination. Je fais … only means 'I go …' when it is with a sport, for example: Je fais de la natation. I go swimming.

Module 6 Vocabulaire

Words I should know for speaking and writing activities

Les matières — *School subjects*
le commerce — *business studies*
le dessin — *art*
le français — *French*
la biologie — *biology*
la chimie — *chemistry*
la géographie — *geography*
la musique — *music*
la physique — *physics*
la religion — *religious studies*
la technologie — *technology*

Had a look ☐ Nearly there ☐ Nailed it ☐

l'allemand (m) — *German*
l'anglais (m) — *English*
l'art dramatique (m) — *drama*
le théâtre — *drama*
l'EPS (f)/le sport — *PE*
l'espagnol (m) — *Spanish*
l'étude des médias (f) — *media studies*
l'histoire (f) — *history*
l'informatique (f) — *ICT*
l'instruction civique (f) — *citizenship*
les arts ménagers (m) — *home technology*
les maths (m) — *maths*

Had a look ☐ Nearly there ☐ Nailed it ☐

L'emploi du temps — *The timetable*
à neuf heures — *at nine o'clock*
à neuf heures dix — *at ten past nine*
à neuf heures et quart — *at a quarter past nine*
à neuf heures et demie — *at half past nine*
à dix heures moins vingt — *at twenty to ten*
à dix heures moins le quart — *at a quarter to ten*
lundi — *(on) Monday(s)*
mardi — *(on) Tuesday(s)*
mercredi — *(on) Wednesday(s)*
jeudi — *(on) Thursday(s)*
vendredi — *(on) Friday(s)*
la récré(ation) — *break time*
l'heure du déjeuner — *lunchtime*
Lundi à neuf heures, j'ai histoire/maths. — *On Monday at nine o'clock, I have history/maths.*
Vendredi, j'ai deux heures de français. — *I have two French lessons on Fridays.*
La récré commence à … — *Break time starts at …*

Had a look ☐ Nearly there ☐ Nailed it ☐

Ce que j'aime et ce que je n'aime pas — *What I like and what I don't like*
Ma matière préférée est … — *My favourite subject is …*
Je suis fort(e) en … — *I am good at …*
Je suis faible en … — *I am weak at …*
Je (ne) suis (pas) doué(e) en … — *I (don't) have a talent for …*
C'est … — *It's …*
facile/difficile — *easy/difficult*
utile/inutile — *useful/useless*
intéressant/ennuyeux — *interesting/boring*
fascinant/passionnant — *fascinating/exciting*
Le/La prof est … — *The teacher is …*
bon(ne) — *good*
marrant(e) — *funny*
sympa — *nice*
gentil(le) — *kind*
sévère — *strict*
impatient(e) — *impatient*
On a trop de devoirs. — *We have too much homework.*

Had a look ☐ Nearly there ☐ Nailed it ☐

Une école bien équipée — *A well-equipped school*
le gymnase — *sports hall*
le hall — *(assembly) hall, auditorium*
le terrain de basket — *basketball court*
le terrain de sport — *sports ground*
la bibliothèque — *library*
la cantine — *canteen*
la cour de récréation — *playground*
la piscine — *swimming pool*
la salle de sport — *gym*
les labos de science (m) — *science labs*
les salles de classe (f) — *classrooms*
les vestiaires (m) — *changing rooms*

Had a look ☐ Nearly there ☐ Nailed it ☐

Mon collège — *My school*
Comment s'appelle ton école? — *What is your school called?*
Mon école s'appelle … — *My school is called …*
C'est quelle sorte d'école? — *What sort of school is it?*
C'est … — *It's …*
une école mixte — *a mixed school*
une école publique — *a state school*
une école privée — *a private school*

35

Module 6 Vocabulaire

une école pour filles/garçons	a school for girls/boys
pour les élèves de 11 à 16 ans	for pupils aged 11 to 16
Il y a combien d'élèves?	How many pupils are there?
Il y a (750) élèves et (45) professeurs.	There are (750) pupils and (45) teachers.
Quels sont les horaires?	What are the school hours?
La journée commence à (8h30) et finit à (16h ou à 17h).	The school day starts at (8.30 a.m.) and finishes at (4 or 5 p.m.).
Il y a combien de cours par jour?	How many lessons are there per day?
Il y a (huit) cours par jour.	There are (eight) lessons per day.
Comment sont les professeurs?	What are the teachers like?
En général, les profs sont gentils/un peu sévères.	In general, teachers are kind/a bit strict.
Qu'est-ce que tu penses de ton collège?	What do you think of your school?
Je pense que les journées sont longues et qu'on a trop de contrôles.	I think the days are long and we have too many tests.

Had a look ☐ Nearly there ☐ Nailed it ☐

L'école chez nous, l'école chez vous — School here and with you

En Grande-Bretagne, …	In Britain …
En France, …	In France …
l'école commence à … et finit à …	school starts at … and finishes at …
on porte un uniforme scolaire	we wear school uniform
ils portent leurs propres habits	they wear their own clothes
on étudie la religion	we study RE
ils n'étudient pas la religion	they don't study RE
on ne redouble pas	we don't repeat a year
ils redoublent	they repeat a year
les grandes vacances durent …	the summer holidays last …
Je préfère le système britannique/français parce que …	I prefer the British/French system because …
le redoublement (n')est (pas) une bonne idée	repeating a year is (not) a good idea
les horaires sont plus raisonnables	the hours are more reasonable
les vacances sont plus longues	the holidays are longer
l'uniforme scolaire est pratique	school uniform is practical

Had a look ☐ Nearly there ☐ Nailed it ☐

Le règlement scolaire — School rules

Il faut être à l'heure.	You must be on time.
Il faut faire ses devoirs.	You have to do your homework.
Il faut porter l'uniforme scolaire.	You have to wear school uniform.
Il est interdit de mâcher du chewing-gum.	It is forbidden to chew gum.
Il est interdit d'utiliser son portable en classe.	It is forbidden to use your mobile phone in class.
Il est interdit de porter des bijoux, des piercings ou trop de maquillage.	It is forbidden to wear jewellery, piercings or too much make-up.
Il est interdit de sortir de l'école pendant l'heure du déjeuner.	It is forbidden to leave school at lunchtime.
Il est interdit de manquer les cours.	It is forbidden to skip lessons.
Je trouve ça …	I think that's …
juste	fair
logique	logical
raisonnable	reasonable
frustrant(e)	frustrating
injuste	unfair
ridicule	ridiculous

Had a look ☐ Nearly there ☐ Nailed it ☐

parce que/car …	because …
c'est/ce n'est pas dangereux	it is/isn't dangerous
c'est/ce n'est pas important	it is/isn't important
on n'est pas des bébés	we aren't babies
il faut respecter les autres	you have to respect other people
la mode/la religion n'a pas de place à l'école	fashion/religion doesn't have any place in school
l'école, c'est pour apprendre	school is for learning

Had a look ☐ Nearly there ☐ Nailed it ☐

L'uniforme scolaire — School uniform

French	English
Je porte …	I wear …
un pantalon	trousers
un polo	a polo shirt
un sweat	a sweatshirt
une chemise	a shirt
une cravate	a tie
une jupe	a skirt
une veste	a blazer/jacket
mes propres vêtements (m)	my own clothes
La mode n'a pas de place à l'école.	Fashion has no place in school.

Module 6 Vocabulaire

French	English
L'uniforme coûte cher.	Uniform is expensive.
Tout le monde se ressemble.	Everyone looks the same/alike.
C'est démodé et embarrassant.	It's old-fashioned and embarrassing.
C'est pratique et confortable.	It's practical and comfortable.

Had a look ☐ Nearly there ☐ Nailed it ☐

À l'école primaire et maintenant / At primary school and now

J'avais …	I had/used to have …
J'ai …	I have …
beaucoup de temps libre	lots of free time
beaucoup d'amis	lots of friends
trop de devoirs	too much homework
J'allais …	I used to go …
Je vais …	I go …
au ciné-club	to film club
au club d'échecs	to chess club
au zoo	to the zoo
à la piscine	to the swimming pool

Had a look ☐ Nearly there ☐ Nailed it ☐

French	English
J'étais …	I was/used to be …
Je suis …	I am …
dans une chorale	in a choir
délégué(e) de classe	class representative
membre de l'équipe de basket	a member of the basketball team
timide	shy
Je faisais …	I used to do/go …
Je fais …	I do/go …
du judo	judo
du karaté	karate
du yoga	yoga
de la danse	dancing
de la natation	swimming

Had a look ☐ Nearly there ☐ Nailed it ☐

Je jouais …	I used to play …
Je joue …	I play …
à cache-cache	hide and seek
au foot	football
au hand	handball
au ping-pong	ping pong, table tennis
au rugby	rugby
Je participais …	I used to participate/take part …

French	English
Je participe … au spectacle de Noël	I participate/take part … in the Christmas play
Je chantais …	I sang …
Je chante … dans la chorale	I sing … in the choir

Had a look ☐ Nearly there ☐ Nailed it ☐

Les succès au collège / Successes at school

Je suis fier/-ière de moi.	I am proud of myself.
Je joue dans l'orchestre.	I play in the orchestra.
Je suis membre du club informatique.	I'm a member of the IT club.
Je suis membre du conseil d'administration.	I'm a member of the school council.
Je vais jouer dans l'équipe de hockey.	I'm going to play in the hockey team.
Je vais participer à un échange scolaire.	I'm going to take part in a school exchange.
J'ai gagné …	I won …
un prix pour mes efforts en classe	a prize for my efforts in class
le championnat de foot/basket	the football/basketball championship
un concours de slam/danse	a slam/dance competition

Had a look ☐ Nearly there ☐ Nailed it ☐

J'ai participé à …	I participated/took part in …
un spectacle	a show
un échange scolaire	a school exchange
une sortie scolaire	a school visit
J'ai organisé …	I organised …
un concert	a concert
un concours de chant	a singing competition
J'ai récolté de l'argent pour une association caritative.	I raised money for a charity.
Les sorties scolaires sont une bonne/mauvaise idée parce que/qu' …	School visits are a good/bad idea because …
on se fait de nouveaux amis	you make new friends
on s'amuse ensemble	you have a laugh together
c'est trop cher/ennuyeux	it's too expensive/boring

Had a look ☐ Nearly there ☐ Nailed it ☐

M6

37

Module 6 Vocabulaire

Extra words I should know for reading and listening activities

Mes matières et mes profs
Mon/Ma prof s'appelle …
Les profs (de maths) sont …
Je le/la/les déteste.
Je l'/les adore.
Je pense que … est (trop/très/assez/un peu) …
C'est amusant/excellent.

My subjects and my teachers
My teacher is called …
The (maths) teachers are …
I hate him/her/them.
I love him/her/them.
I think that … is (too/very/quite/a little) …
It is fun/excellent.

Had a look ☐ Nearly there ☐ Nailed it ☐

Dans mon collège
Il y a (environ) …
Malheureusement, il n'y a pas de …
des salles de classes modernes (f)
un grand choix de …
un labo(ratoire) de langues/sciences
Les vestiaires/les toilettes sont sales/sont pleins de …
Je le/la/les trouve bien/utile(s)/cool/bien aménagé(es).

In my school
There is/are (about) …
Unfortunately, there isn't/aren't …
modern classrooms
a great choice of …
a language/science laboratory
The changing rooms/toilets are dirty/full of …
I think it is/they are good/useful/cool/well-equipped.

Had a look ☐ Nearly there ☐ Nailed it ☐

Les études en Angleterre et en France
La récré est à … et dure … minutes.
Il y a … cours par jour/élèves/contrôles.
Il n'y a pas cours le …
On a … heure(s) pour le déjeuner.
On a trop de …
Les journées/cours sont (trop) …
un lycée
En sixième/cinquième/quatrième/troisième/seconde*/première*/terminale*
à l'âge de … ans

Studying in France and in England
Break starts at … and lasts … minutes.
There are … lessons per day/pupils/tests.
There are no lessons on …
We have … hour(s) for lunch.
We have too many …
The days/lessons are (too) …
a high school (Yr 11-13 only)
In Yr 7/8/9/10/11/12/13

at the age of … years old

S'ils ne font pas assez de progrès, ils redoublent**.
Les élèves passent leur brevet du collège/baccalauréat/en classe supérieure.
Les élèves continuent leurs études à l'université.

If they do not make enough progress, they repeat the year.
The pupils take their GCSEs/A Levels/move up to the next class.
The pupils continue their studies at university.

Had a look ☐ Nearly there ☐ Nailed it ☐

L'uniforme scolaire
le jean
le jogging
le pull
le tee-shirt
La mode/L'uniforme coûte cher.
La mode n'a pas de place …
se ressembler
Je (ne) voudrais (pas) …
C'est démodé.
C'est pratique.
C'est confortable.
C'est embarrassant.

School uniform
jeans
jogging pants
a jumper
t-shirt
Fashion/The uniform is expensive.
Fashion has no place …
to look like each other
I would (not) like …
It's old-fashioned.
It's practical.
It's confortable.
It's embarrassing.

Had a look ☐ Nearly there ☐ Nailed it ☐

La vie extra-scolaire
l'orchestre (m)
faire du théâtre/beaucoup de clubs
aller à la piscine municipale

After-school activities
the orchestra
to do drama/lots of clubs
to go to the local pool

Had a look ☐ Nearly there ☐ Nailed it ☐

En échange
On se fait de nouveaux amis.
On améliore ses compétences en langue.
On habite chez une famille d'une culture différente.
On visite un nouveau pays/une nouvelle région.
On apprécie (non seulement) les différences mais (aussi) les similarités.

On an exchange
You make new friends.
Your language skills get better.
You live with a family from another culture.
You visit a new country/a new region.
You appreciate (not just) the differences but (also) the similarities.

Module 6 Vocabulaire

nos correspondant(e)(s)	our penfriend(s)
On est en route pour …	We are on the way to …
Hier, j'ai vomi.	Yesterday, I was sick.
La mer était vraiment agitée.	The sea was really rough.
On prend le train pour aller à (Londres).	We are getting the train to go to (London).
Nous sommes dans (une fôret).	We are in (a forest).
On fait du tir à l'arc.	We are doing archery.
On va faire (du segway).	We are going to go (on a segway).
La famille (anglaise) s'occupe bien de moi.	The (English) family are looking after me well.
J'avais peur …	I was scared …
C'était super/rigolo/top!	It was great/funny/the best!
J'ai acheté de beaux cadeaux pour vous!	I have bought some beautiful presents for you!
Quand on partira, je serai triste!	When we leave, I will be sad!
On va rester en contact sur Facebook.	We will stay in touch on Facebook.

Had a look ☐ **Nearly there** ☐ **Nailed it** ☐

Le succès au collège	**Success at school**
On va organiser une soirée disco pour les sixièmes.	We are going to organise a disco evening for the Year 7 pupils.
Ça va être un grand succès!	It's going to be a great success!
Au début de l'année …	At the start of the year …
On a organisé un concours de slam!	We organised a 'slam' competition!
On a joué contre une équipe de …	We played against a team from …
On a gagné le match!	We won the match!
Je suis resté(e) chez …	I stayed at …'s house.
une sortie scolaire	a school trip
On a voyagé …	We travelled …
On a visité …	We visited …

Had a look ☐ **Nearly there** ☐ **Nailed it** ☐

M 6

⭐ *Watch out for false friends such as *seconde*, *première* and *terminale*. In the context of school, all of these words have very specific meanings: Year 11, Year 12 and Year 13.

⭐ **Redoubler in a school context does not mean 'to redouble'. It conveys the idea of repeating a school year, which is something French pupils have to do if they don't make sufficient progress over the year! It is important that you learn how the French education system works as it is very different to the English one.

39

Module 7 Vocabulaire

Words I should know for speaking and writing activities

Les métiers	Jobs
Je suis/Il/Elle est …	I am/He/She is a/an …
Je veux être …	I want to be a/an …
Je veux travailler comme …	I want to work as a/an …
avocat/avocate	lawyer
ingénieur/ingénieure	engineer
électricien/électricienne	electrician
mécanicien/mécanicienne	mechanic
musicien/musicienne	musician
maçon/maçonne	builder
patron/patronne	boss
coiffeur/coiffeuse	hairdresser
programmeur/programmeuse	computer programmer
serveur/serveuse	waiter/waitress
vendeur/vendeuse	salesperson
acteur/actrice	actor/actress
agriculteur/agricultrice	farmer
créateur/créatrice de mode	fashion designer
créateur/créatrice de jeux vidéo	video game designer
directeur/directrice d'entreprise	company director
facteur/factrice	postman/woman

Had a look ☐ Nearly there ☐ Nailed it ☐

instituteur/institutrice	primary school teacher
boucher/bouchère	butcher
boulanger/boulangère	baker
fermier/fermière	farmer
infirmier/infirmière	nurse
pompier/pompière	firefighter
architecte	architect
chef de cuisine	chef
comptable	accountant
dentiste	dentist
journaliste	journalist
pilote	pilot
secrétaire	secretary
vétérinaire	vet
agent de police	policeman/woman
médecin	doctor
professeur	teacher
soldat	soldier

Had a look ☐ Nearly there ☐ Nailed it ☐

Lieux de travail	Workplaces
Je travaille/Il/Elle travaille …	I work/He/She works …
dans un bureau	in an office
dans un commissariat de police	in a police station
dans un collège	in a secondary school
dans un garage	in a garage
dans un hôpital	in a hospital
dans un magasin	in a shop
dans un restaurant	in a restaurant
dans un salon de coiffure	in a hair salon
dans une boulangerie	in a bakery
dans une école primaire	in a primary school
dans une ferme	on a farm
à bord d'un avion	on a plane

Had a look ☐ Nearly there ☐ Nailed it ☐

Les passions	Passions
Ma passion, c'est …	My passion is …
la cuisine/la mode	cooking/fashion
le sport/le théâtre	sport/theatre/drama
les ordinateurs (m)/les voitures (f)	computers/cars

Had a look ☐ Nearly there ☐ Nailed it ☐

J'aimerais …	I would like to …
Je voudrais/J'aimerais travailler …	I would like to work …
dans un bureau	in an office
dans un magasin	in a shop
en plein air	outside
avec des enfants	with children
avec des animaux	with animals
avec des ordinateurs	with computers
seul(e)	alone, on my own
en équipe	in a team
à l'étranger	abroad
Je voudrais faire un métier …	I would like to do a … job
créatif	creative
manuel	manual
à responsabilité	responsible, with responsibility/management

Had a look ☐ Nearly there ☐ Nailed it ☐

Tu voudrais travailler dans quel secteur et pourquoi?	What area would you like to work in and why?
Je voudrais travailler dans …	I would like to work in …
le sport et les loisirs	sport and leisure
le commerce	business
la médecine et la santé	medicine and health

Module 7 Vocabulaire

l'audiovisuel et les médias	audiovisual and media
l'informatique et les télécommunications	IT and telecommunications
l'hôtellerie et la restauration	the hotel and catering industry

Had a look ☐ Nearly there ☐ Nailed it ☐

Je suis …	I am …
indépendant(e)	independent
intelligent(e)	intelligent
motivé(e)	motivated
(bien) organisé(e)	(well-)organised
actif/-ve	active
créatif/-ve	creative
ambitieux/-euse	ambitious
sérieux/-euse	serious
travailleur/-euse	hard-working
sociable	sociable
timide	shy
J'aime …	I like …
le contact avec les gens	(having) contact with people
travailler en équipe	working in a team
J'aimerais avoir un métier bien payé.	I would like to have a well-paid job.

Had a look ☐ Nearly there ☐ Nailed it ☐

Mes projets d'avenir — My plans for the future

Je veux/J'espère/Je voudrais …	I want/I hope/I would like …
passer mes examens	to take my exams
réussir mes examens	to pass my exams
prendre une année sabbatique	to take a gap year
voyager/visiter d'autres pays	to travel/to visit other countries
faire un apprentissage/devenir apprenti(e)	to do an apprenticeship/to become an apprentice
aller à l'université/continuer mes études à la fac(ulté)	to go to university/to continue my studies at university
faire du bénévolat/du travail bénévole	to do voluntary work
me marier ou me pacser	to get married or enter into a civil partnership
avoir des enfants	to have children
habiter/m'installer avec mon copain/ma copine	to live/move in with my boyfriend/girlfriend

Had a look ☐ Nearly there ☐ Nailed it ☐

Tu parles quelles langues? — Which languages do you speak?

Je parle couramment …	I speak … fluently.
Je parle assez/très bien …	I speak … quite/very well.
Je parle un peu …	I speak a little …
Je parle seulement …	I only speak …
Je parle mal …	I speak … badly.
… est ma langue maternelle.	… is my native language/mother tongue.
J'apprends (actuellement) …	I am (currently) learning …
l'allemand (m)	German
l'anglais (m)	English
l'arabe (m)	Arabic
l'espagnol (m)	Spanish
le français	French
le gujarati	Gujarati
le hindi	Hindi
l'italien (m)	Italian
le japonais	Japanese
le mandarin	Mandarin
l'ourdou (m)	Urdu
le polonais	Polish
le portugais	Portuguese
le roumain	Romanian
le russe	Russian

Had a look ☐ Nearly there ☐ Nailed it ☐

Comment utilises-tu des langues étrangères? — How do you use foreign languages?

J'utilise des langues étrangères …	I use foreign languages …
pour faire des réservations par téléphone	to make reservations on the phone
pour écrire des e-mails	to write emails
pour parler avec des clients et des collègues à l'étranger	to speak to customers and colleagues abroad
pour commander quelque chose à manger	to order something to eat
pour demander mon chemin	to ask for directions
pour communiquer avec des clients qui ne parlent pas le français	to communicate with customers who don't speak French
pour faire des annonces	to make announcements
pour donner des renseignements aux passagers	to give information to passengers
pour aider des touristes et répondre à leurs questions	to help tourists and answer their questions

Had a look ☐ Nearly there ☐ Nailed it ☐

M7

41

Module 7 Vocabulaire

Gagner de l'argent — *Earning money*
Tu as un petit boulot? — *Do you have a part-time job?*
Que fais-tu pour gagner de l'argent? — *What do you do to earn money?*
J'aide à la maison. — *I help at home.*
Je passe l'aspirateur. — *I do the vacuuming.*
Je fais la vaisselle. — *I do the dishes.*
Je lave la voiture (de mon père). — *I wash the car (my dad's car).*
Je tonds la pelouse (de mes grands-parents). — *I mow the lawn (my grandparents' lawn).*
Je promène le chien. — *I walk the dog.*
J'ai un petit boulot. — *I have a part-time job.*
Je sers les clients. — *I serve customers.*
Je remplis les rayons. — *I stack the shelves.*
Je fais du baby-sitting (pour mes voisins). — *I babysit (for my neighbours).*
Je livre des journaux. — *I deliver newspapers.*
Je gagne/Je reçois … — *I earn/I receive/get …*
Mon père/Ma mère me donne … — *My father/mother gives me …*
Mes parents me donnent … — *My parents give me …*
quinze euros/dix livres … — *fifteen euros/ten pounds …*
… par heure/jour/semaine/mois — *… per hour/day/week/month*

Had a look ☐ Nearly there ☐ Nailed it ☐

Postuler à un emploi — *Applying for a job*
une annonce — *an advert*
on recherche … — *we are looking for …*
les responsabilités (f) — *responsibilities*
les qualifications (f) — *qualifications*
les compétences (f) — *skills*
l'expérience (f) — *experience*
les atouts (m) — *strengths*
remplir un CV — *to fill in a CV*
écrire une lettre de motivation — *to write a covering letter*
faire une vidéo — *to make a video*

Had a look ☐ Nearly there ☐ Nailed it ☐

Mon stage — *My work experience*
J'ai fait un stage … — *I did work experience …*
dans un bureau — *in an office*
dans un garage — *in a garage*
dans un hôtel — *in a hotel*
dans un magasin de mode — *in a clothes shop*
dans un salon de coiffure — *in a hairdressing salon*
dans une banque — *in a bank*
J'ai servi les clients. — *I served customers.*
J'ai rangé les vêtements. — *I tidied the clothes.*
J'ai aidé les mécaniciens. — *I helped the mechanics.*
J'ai appris à changer des pneus. — *I learned to change tyres.*
J'ai tapé des documents. — *I typed documents.*
J'ai fait des photocopies. — *I made photocopies.*
J'ai lavé les cheveux des clients. — *I washed customers' hair.*
J'ai fait du café. — *I made coffee.*
J'ai passé l'aspirateur. — *I did the vacuuming.*
J'ai répondu au téléphone. — *I answered the phone.*
J'ai fait des réservations. — *I made bookings.*
J'ai envoyé des e-mails. — *I sent emails.*

Had a look ☐ Nearly there ☐ Nailed it ☐

C'était une bonne expérience? — *Was it a good experience?*
C'était … — *It was …*
amusant/bien — *fun/good*
génial/intéressant — *great/interesting*
passionnant — *exciting*
une bonne expérience — *a good experience*
difficile/ennuyeux — *difficult/boring*
fatigant/monotone — *tiring/monotonous*
(complètement) nul — *(completely) rubbish*
une mauvaise expérience — *a bad experience*
Mon patron/Ma patronne était … gentil(le)/trop sévère. — *My boss was … kind/too strict.*
Mes collègues (n')étaient (pas) (très) sympa. — *My colleagues were (not) (very) nice.*
J'ai beaucoup appris. — *I learned a lot.*
Je n'ai rien appris. — *I didn't learn anything.*

Had a look ☐ Nearly there ☐ Nailed it ☐

Module 7 Vocabulaire

Extra words I should know for reading and listening activities

Les qualités personnelles	Personal qualities
en bonne forme	fit
fort(e)	strong
patient(e)	patient
calme	calm
sociable	sociable
heureux/-euse	happy

Had a look ☐ **Nearly there** ☐ **Nailed it** ☐

L'avenir	The future
un métier fascinant/passionnant	a fascinating/exciting job
Tu peux sauver la vie des gens!	You can save people's lives!
Tu peux devenir célèbre!	You can become famous!
Pourquoi ne pas devenir … ?*	Why not become … ?
Pense à être …	Think of being …
Aimerais-tu être … ?*	Would you like to be … ?
Je prendrai …	I will take …
J'irai …	I will go …
J'aurai …	I will have …
Je serai …*	I will be …
Je trouverai …	I will find …
Je me marierai …	I will get married …
l'homme/la femme de mes rêves	the man/woman of my dreams
ma propre entreprise	my own business
le tour du monde**	tour of the world
la fac(ulté)	uni(versity)
Médecins Sans Frontières	Charity group that offers medical care in crisis/war situations
Ce sera génial!	It will be great!

Had a look ☐ **Nearly there** ☐ **Nailed it** ☐

Le mariage	Marriage
la cérémonie	the ceremony
l'église (f)	the church
mon futur mari/ma future femme	my future husband/wife
être marié(e)(s) depuis … ans	to be married for … years
habiter ensemble	to live together
pour voir si ça marche	to see if it works out
fonder une famille	to start a family

Had a look ☐ **Nearly there** ☐ **Nailed it** ☐

Pour gagner de l'argent …	To earn money …
Je fais ça gratuitement.	I do that for free.
chaque semaine	every week
quand il/elle n'est pas là	when he/she isn't there
pendant les grandes vacances	during the summer holidays
de temps en temps	from time to time
les activités (f)	activities
J'ai déjà un peu d'expérience de …	I already have a little experience of …
postuler au poste de …	to apply for the post/position of …

Had a look ☐ **Nearly there** ☐ **Nailed it** ☐

Les expériences récentes	Recent experiences
J'ai travaillé …	I worked …
J'ai supervisé …	I supervised …
J'ai décidé de …	I decided to …
J'ai commencé à …	I started to …
Mon travail consiste à …	My job consists of …
Les horaires sont (un peu) longs.	The days/The working hours are (a little) long.

Had a look ☐ **Nearly there** ☐ **Nailed it** ☐

⭐ *Remember **not** to use an article after a verb (conjugated or in the infinitive form) when you are talking about a job.

Examples

Pourquoi ne pas devenir pilote?	Why not become a pilot?
Aimerais-tu être chanteuse?	Would you like to be a singer?
Je serai prof.	I will be a teacher.

Jobs in French usually have masculine and feminine versions of their spellings but not all.

⭐ **Some nouns in French change their meaning, depending on whether they are used in the masculine or feminine form.

le Tour de France the Tour de France (cycle race)

la tour Eiffel the Eiffel Tower

43

Module 8 Vocabulaire

Words I should know for speaking and writing activities

Ce qui est important pour moi / *What's important to me*

Ce qui est important pour moi, c'est …	*What's important to me is …*
l'argent (m)	*money*
le sport	*sport*
la musique	*music*
ma famille	*my family*
ma santé	*my health*
mes amis (m)	*my friends*
mes animaux (m)	*my animals*
mes études (f)	*my studies*

Had a look ☐ Nearly there ☐ Nailed it ☐

Ce qui me préoccupe / *What concerns me*

Ce qui me préoccupe, c'est …	*What concerns me is …*
l'environnement (m)	*the environment*
l'état (m) de la planète	*the state of the planet*
le racisme	*racism*
la cruauté envers les animaux	*cruelty to animals*
la faim	*hunger*
la guerre	*war*
l'injustice (f)	*injustice*
la pauvreté	*poverty*
la violence	*violence*

Had a look ☐ Nearly there ☐ Nailed it ☐

Qu'est-ce qu'on peut faire pour aider? / *What can we do to help?*

On peut faire du bénévolat.	*You can do voluntary work.*
On peut parrainer un enfant.	*You can sponsor a child.*
On peut donner de l'argent à une association caritative.	*You can give money to a charity.*
On peut recycler.	*You can recycle.*
Il faut agir.	*You/We have to act.*
Il faut lutter contre la faim.	*You/We have to fight against hunger.*
Il faut signer des pétitions.	*You/We have to sign petitions.*
Il faut participer à des manifestations.	*You/We have to take part in demonstrations.*
Il faut éduquer les gens.	*You/We have to educate people.*

Had a look ☐ Nearly there ☐ Nailed it ☐

Quel temps fera-t-il? / *What will the weather be like?*

Il y aura …	*There will be …*
de la pluie	*rain*
de la neige	*snow*
du vent	*wind*
du tonnerre	*thunder*
des averses (f)	*showers*
des éclairs (m)	*lightning*
des éclaircies (f)	*sunny intervals*
Il fera …	*It/The weather will be …*
beau	*nice, good*
mauvais	*bad*
chaud	*hot*
froid	*cold*
frais	*chilly*
Le temps sera …	*The weather will be …*
ensoleillé	*sunny*
nuageux	*cloudy*
orageux	*stormy*

Had a look ☐ Nearly there ☐ Nailed it ☐

Les problèmes environnementaux / *Environmental problems*

Le plus grand problème environnemental, c'est …	*The biggest environmental problem is …*
le changement climatique	*climate change*
le manque d'eau potable	*the lack of drinking water*
la disparition des espèces	*the extinction of species*
la destruction des forêts tropicales	*the destruction of the rainforests*
la surpopulation	*overpopulation*
la pollution de l'air	*air pollution*
la sécheresse	*drought*
les inondations (f)	*flooding, floods*
les incendies (m)	*fires*
Les arbres nous donnent de l'oxygène et nous les coupons tous les jours.	*Trees give us oxygen, and every day we cut them down.*
Beaucoup de personnes n'ont pas accès à cette ressource vitale.	*Lots of people don't have access to this vital resource.*
On détruit la planète.	*We are destroying the planet.*
C'est très inquiétant.	*It's very worrying.*
C'est catastrophique.	*It's catastrophic.*

Had a look ☐ Nearly there ☐ Nailed it ☐

Que doit-on faire pour sauver notre planète? / *What should we do to save our planet?*

On doit/On peut …	*You/We should/can …*
recycler	*recycle*
trier les déchets	*separate/sort the rubbish*
faire du compost	*make compost*

44

Module 8 Vocabulaire

French	English
consommer moins d'énergie	consume less energy
éteindre les appareils électriques et la lumière	turn off electrical appliances and the light
mettre un pullover au lieu d'allumer le chauffage	put on a jumper instead of turning on the heating
faire des achats responsables	make responsible purchases
utiliser du papier recyclé	use recycled paper
acheter des produits verts et des produits bio	buy green and organic products

Had a look ☐ Nearly there ☐ Nailed it ☐

voyager autrement	travel differently
utiliser les transports en commun	use public transport
aller au collège à vélo	go to school by bike
réutiliser	reuse
refuser les sacs en plastique	turn down plastic bags
avoir une bouteille d'eau au lieu de prendre un gobelet jetable	have a bottle of water instead of taking a disposable cup
économiser l'eau	save water
boire l'eau du robinet	drink tap water
prendre une douche au lieu de prendre un bain	take a shower instead of a bath
tirer la chasse d'eau moins fréquemment	flush the toilet less frequently
fermer le robinet en se lavant les dents	turn off the tap while brushing your teeth
installer des panneaux solaires	install solar panels

Had a look ☐ Nearly there ☐ Nailed it ☐

D'où vient ton tee-shirt? / Where does your T-shirt come from?

Les produits pas chers sont souvent fabriqués dans des conditions de travail inacceptables.	Cheap products are often made in unacceptable working conditions.
Les ouvriers sont sous-payés.	The workers are underpaid.
Leur journée de travail est trop longue.	Their working day is too long.
Il faut/On doit …	We must …
forcer les grandes marques à garantir un salaire minimum	force big brands to guarantee a minimum wage
acheter des produits issus du commerce équitable	buy fair trade products
acheter des vêtements fabriqués en France/au Royaume-Uni	buy clothes that are made in France/in the UK

réfléchir à l'impact sur l'environnement	think about the impact on the environment
essayer de respecter l'homme et l'environnement à la fois	try to respect people and the environment at the same time

Had a look ☐ Nearly there ☐ Nailed it ☐

Faire du bénévolat / Doing volunteer work

Tu peux/J'aimerais …	You can/I would like …
travailler avec des personnes âgées	to work with elderly people
travailler avec des enfants	to work with children
travailler avec des sans-abri/des SDF	to work with homeless people
travailler avec des animaux	to work with animals
participer à un projet de conservation	to participate in a conservation project
Je fais du bénévolat parce que …	I do volunteer work because …
pour moi, c'est important d'aider les autres	for me, it's important to help other people
pour moi, c'est important de participer à la vie en société	for me, it's important to participate in society
j'aime développer de nouvelles compétences	I like developing new skills
j'aime rencontrer de nouvelles personnes	I like meeting new people
c'est une expérience enrichissante pour moi	it's a rewarding experience for me
ça me donne plus confiance en moi	it gives me more confidence in myself

Had a look ☐ Nearly there ☐ Nailed it ☐

Je travaille avec …	I work with …
J'aide un enfant avec ses devoirs.	I help a child with his homework.
Je participe à …	I participate in …
Je suis membre de l'organisation …	I am a member of the organisation …
Je travaille dans un refuge.	I work in a refuge/shelter.
Je parle/discute avec …	I talk to …
Je promène les chiens.	I walk the dogs.

Had a look ☐ Nearly there ☐ Nailed it ☐

Les grands événements / Big events

Cet événement/Ce genre d'événement … attire les touristes	This event/This type of event … attracts tourists

M8

45

Module 8 Vocabulaire

encourage la pratique du sport	encourages participation in sport
donne des modèles aux jeunes	gives young people role models
permet aux gens de s'amuser	allows people to have a good time
unit les gens	unites people
L'année dernière/L'été dernier, …	Last year/Last summer, …
je suis allé(e) à un festival/à la Coupe du Monde	I went to a festival/to the World Cup
j'ai vu (le Tour de France)	I saw (the Tour de France)
C'est …	It's …
un événement qui est connu dans le monde entier	an event that is known throughout the world
le plus grand festival (de théâtre) au monde	the biggest (theatre) festival in the world
Il y a une ambiance magique!	There is a magical atmosphere!
Il a lieu/Ça se passe (à Nice/en février).	It takes place (in Nice/in February).
L'été prochain/L'année prochaine, …	Next summer/Next year, …
je vais y retourner	I am going to go back there
je vais aller à …	I am going to go to …
je vais encore regarder …	I am going to watch … again

Had a look ☐ **Nearly there** ☐ **Nailed it** ☐

Module 8 Vocabulaire

Extra words I should know for reading and listening activities

Le climat de notre planète	***Our planet's climate***	fabriquer dans une usine	*to make in a factory*
Il y aura (plus/moins de) soleil/pluie/vent/neige/ tempêtes tropicales.	*There will be (more/less) sun/rain/wind/snow/ tropical storms.*	repartir pour le motif imprimé(e)	*to set off back to slogan printed*
un (très violent) cyclone/ouragan*	*a (very violent) cyclone/ hurricane*	Tu portes le tee-shirt pendant un moment …	*You wear the T-shirt for a while …*
le changement climatique au cours du XXIe siècle	*climate change over the course of the 21st century*	Tu donnes le tee-shirt à une association caritative.	*You give the T-shirt to a charity.*
la température globale	*global temperature*	vendu à un prix favorable	*sold at a good price*
les conséquences (f) causer d'énormes destructions et plusieurs morts	*the consequences to cause massive destruction and several deaths*	les gens dans les pays pauvres avoir quelque chose de qualité	*people in poor countries to have something of quality*
frapper	*to strike, to hit*	Évitons la pollution!**	*Let's avoid pollution!*
le Pacifique sud	*the southern Pacific Ocean*	Had a look ☐ Nearly there ☐ Nailed it ☐	
contaminer	*to pollute*		
une ressource vitale	*a vital resource*	**Le bénévolat**	***Voluntary work***
recycler le verre/carton/ papier	*to recycle glass/ cardboard/paper*	planter des arbres le froid	*to plant trees the cold*
allumer rarement le chauffage	*to rarely put the heating on*	la solitude	*loneliness*
être membre d'une équipe verte	*to be a member of an environmental team*	Had a look ☐ Nearly there ☐ Nailed it ☐	
installer des panneaux solaires	*to put in solar panels*	**Les grands événements**	***Big events***
Had a look ☐ Nearly there ☐ Nailed it ☐		Ce genre d'événement encourage la pratique du sport.	*This kind of event encourages people to do sport.*
Les produits verts?	***Environmentally friendly products?***	le festival d'Édimbourg deux années de suite	*the Edinburgh festival two years in a row*
Le coton est cultivé …	*The cotton is grown …*	Had a look ☐ Nearly there ☐ Nailed it ☐	
Le coton est une plante.	*Cotton is a plant.*		
Les balles de coton sont transportées/chargées/ exportées/transformées/ envoyées … en tissu	*The cotton balls are transported/loaded/ exported/transformed/ sent … into material*		

⭐ *Take extra care with words that are very similar to words in English, for example:

l'ouragan	hurricane
le vent	wind
le gel	frost

⭐ **The *nous* form of the verb in the imperative tense is often used to convey the idea of doing something collectively.

Évitons la pollution! Let's avoid pollution!

M 8

47

ISBN 978-1-292-17257-6